English - Arabic

My first Picture Dictionary

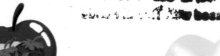

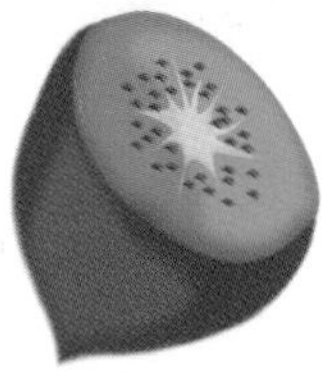

Designed and edited by : Maria Watson
Translated by : Dr. Amir Jamal

Biblio Bee Publicati

English - Arabic
My First Picture Dictionary

ISBN: 978 1 908357 74 8

Published by
Biblio Bee Publications
An imprint of **ibs BOOKS (UK)**
56, Langland Crescent, Stanmore HA7 1NG, U.K.
Tel: 020 8900 2640, Fax: 020 3621 6116,
email: sales@starbooksuk.com, www.starbooksuk.com

First Edition : 2016
Reprint : 2017

Printed at : Star Print-O-Bind, New Delhi-110 020 (India)

This dictionary has been published in the following languages:
Arabic, Bengali, Chinese, Croatian, Farsi, French, Gujarati, Hindi, Latvian, Lithuanian, Pashto, Polish, Portuguese, Punjabi, Romanian, Russian, Spanish, Tamil and Urdu.

Aa

actor

mumaththil مُمَثِّل

actress

mumaththilah مُمَثِّلَة

adult

bāligh بَالِغ

aeroplane
US English **airplane**

ṭā'irah طَائِرَة

air conditioner

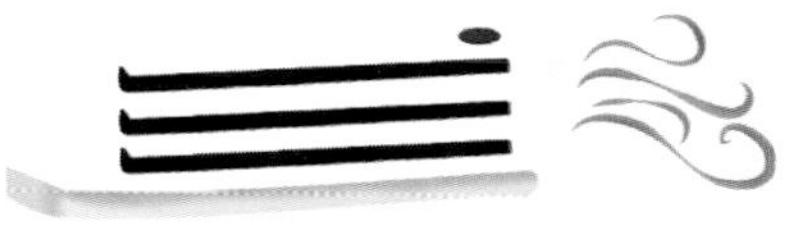

مُكَيِّفُ الْهَوَاء
mukayyiful-hawā'

air hostess
US English **flight attendant**

muḍīfah مُضِيْفَة

airport

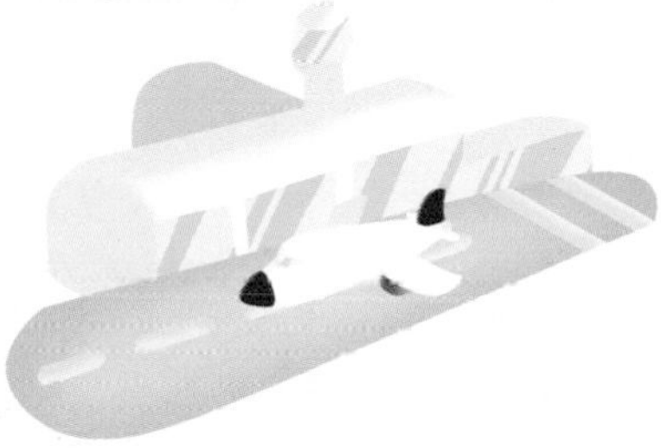

maṭār مَطَار

album

'albūm أَلْبُوْم

almond

lauz لَوْز

alphabet

ḥurūful hijā' حُرُوْفُ الْهِجَاء

ambulance

سَيَّارَةُ الإِسْعَاف
sayyāratul 'is'āf

a b c d e f g h i j k l m n o p q r s t u v w x y z

angel

malak مَلَك

animal

ḥayawān حَيَوان

ankle

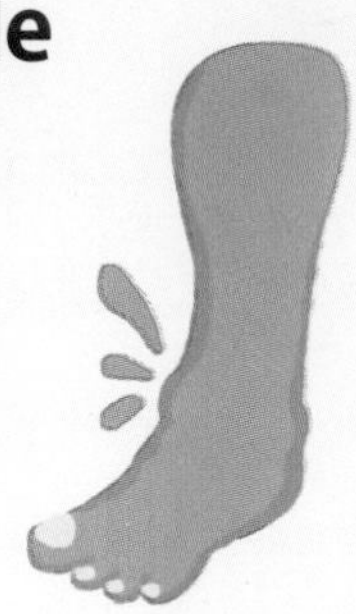

kāḥil\kaʿb كاحِل/كَعْب

ant

namlah نَمْلَة

antelope

ẓab-y ظَبْي

antenna

hawāʾiyy هَوائِيّ

apartment

shuqqah شُقَّة

ape

qird قِرْد

apple

tuffāḥ تُفّاح

apricot

mishmish مِشْمِش

apron

miʾzar مِئْزَر

aquarium

حَوْضُ السَّمَك
ḥauḍus samak

archery
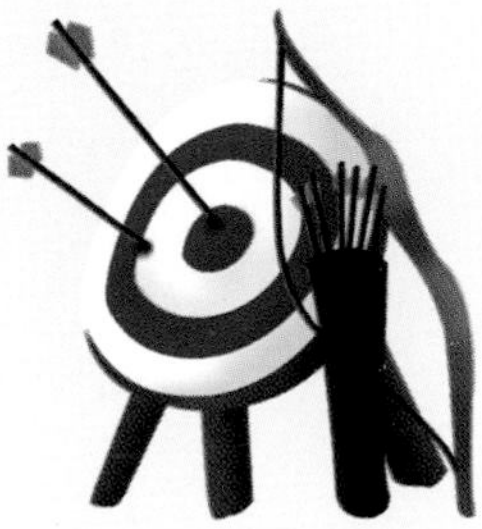

rimāyah رِمَايَة

architect

مُهَنْدِس مِعْمَارِيّ
muhandis miʿmāriyy

arm
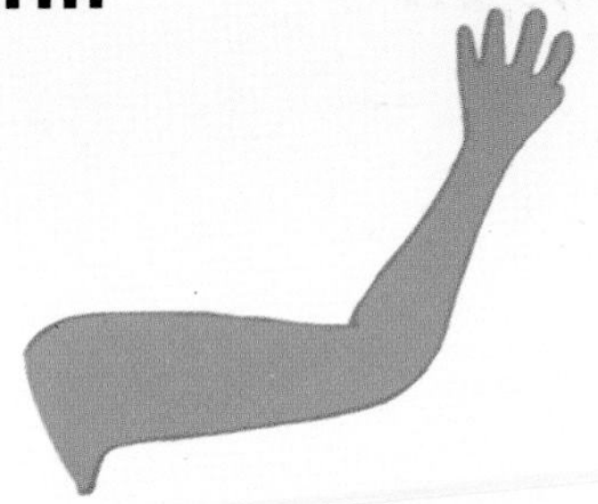

dhirāʿ ذِرَاع

armour
US English **armor**

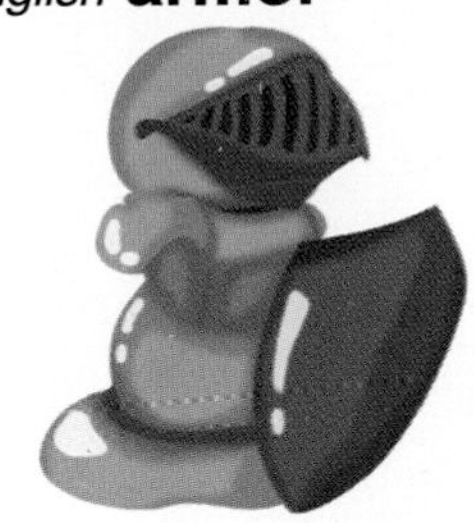

dirʿ دِرْع

arrow

sahm سَهْم

artist

rassām رَسَّام

asparagus
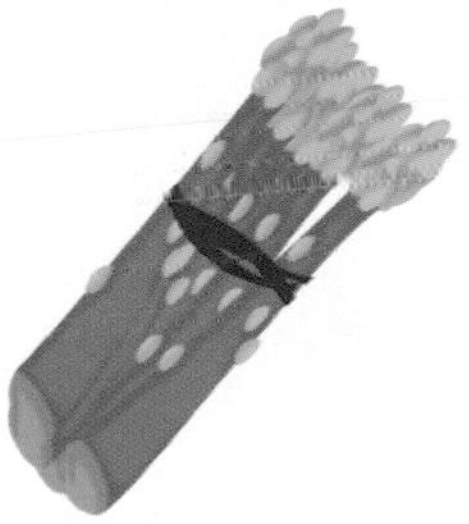

al-hilyaun الْهِلْيَوْن

astronaut

faḍāʾiyy فَضَائِيّ

astronomer

falakiyy فَلَكِيّ

athlete

لَاعِب رِيَاضِيّ
lāʿib riyāḍiyy

atlas
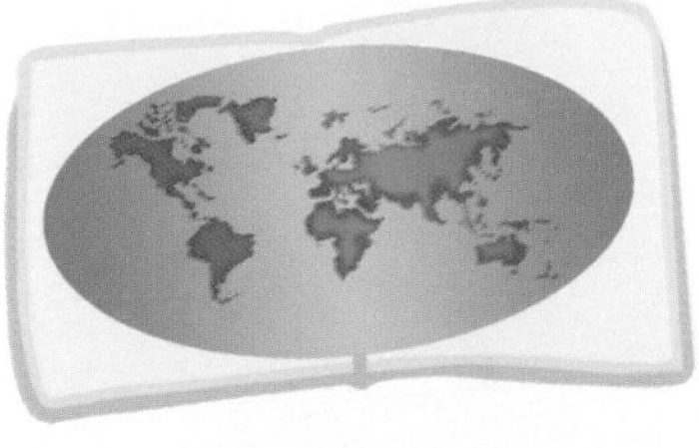

ʾatlas أَطْلَس

aunt

khālah خَالَة

a b c d e f g h i j k l m n o p q r s t u v w x y z

author

mu'allif مُؤَلِّف

automobile

sayyārah سَيَّارَة

autumn

kharīf خَرِيف

avalanche

hayār thaljiyy هَيَار ثَلْجِيّ

award

jā'izah, ka's جَائِزَة، كَأْس

axe

fa's فَأْس

baby

ṭifl طِفْل

back

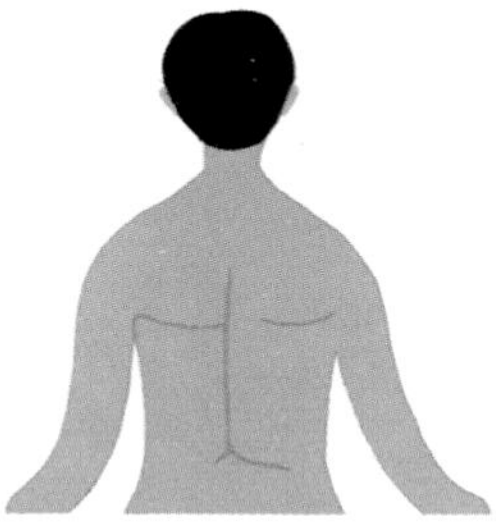

ẓahr ظَهْر

bacon

laḥmu khinzīr لَحْمُ خِنْزِير

badge

wisām وِسَام

badminton

tinisur rīshah تِنِسُ الرِّيْشَة

bag
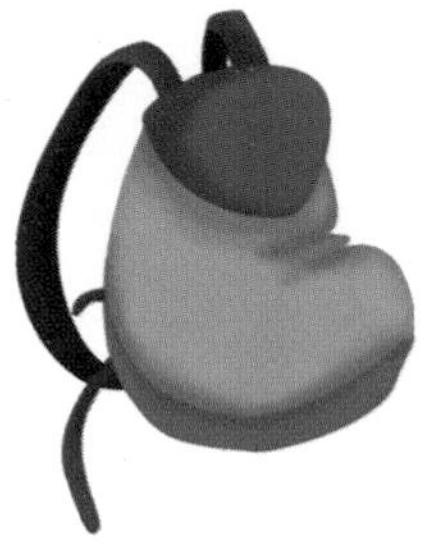

ḥaqībah حَقِيْبَة

baker

khabbāz خَبَّاز

balcony
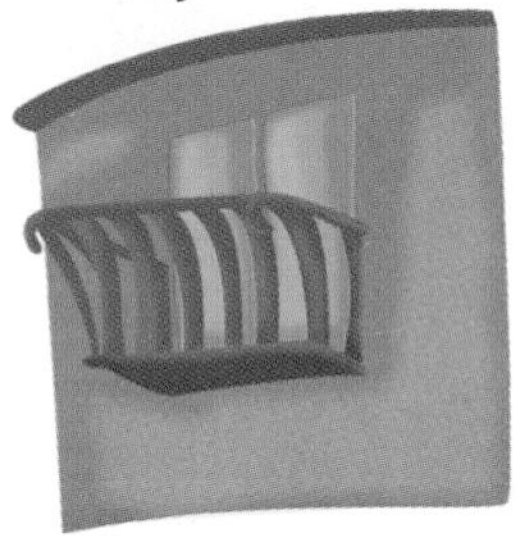

balkūn بَلْكُوْن

bald

ʼaṣlaʻ أَصْلَع

ball

kurah كُرَة

ballerina

رَاقِصَةُ بَالِيْه
rāqiṣatu bālīh

balloon
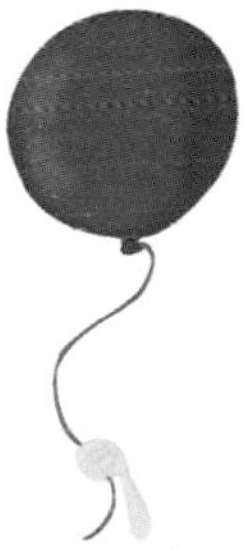

bālūn بَالُوْن

bamboo

khaizurān خَيْزُرَان

banana
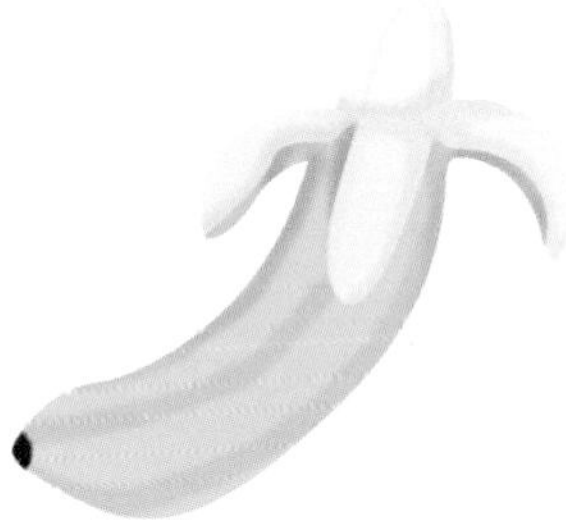

mauz مَوْز

band

فِرْقَة (مُوْسِيْقِيَّة)
firqah (mūsīqiyyah)

bandage
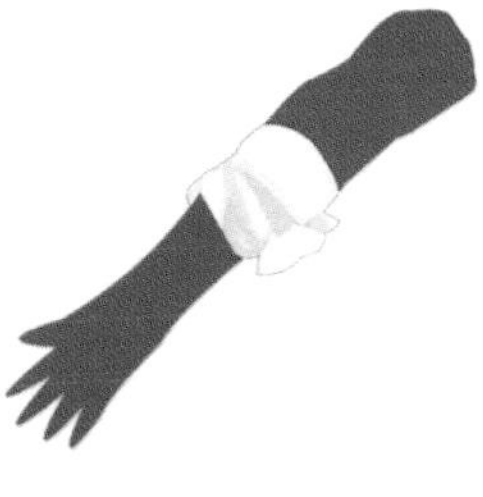

ḍimādah ضِمَادَة

barbeque

shiwāʼ شِوَاء

a b c d e f g h i j k l m n o p q r s t u v w x y z

a b c d e f g h i j k l m n o p q r s t u v w x y z

barn

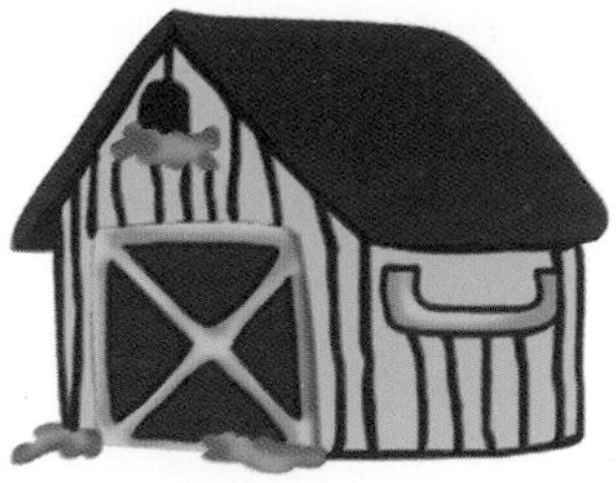

مَخْزَنُ الْحُبُوْب
makhzanul ḥubūb

barrel

barmīl بَرْمِيْل

baseball

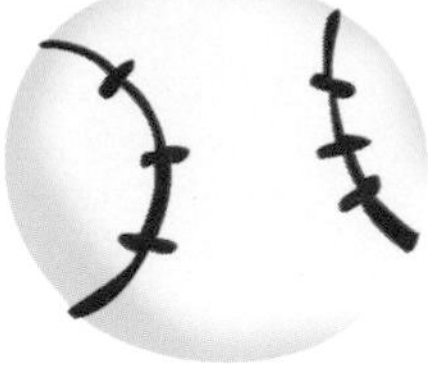

bīsbūl بِيْسْبُوْل

basket

sallah سَلَّة

basketball

kuratus sallah كُرَةُ السَّلَّة

bat

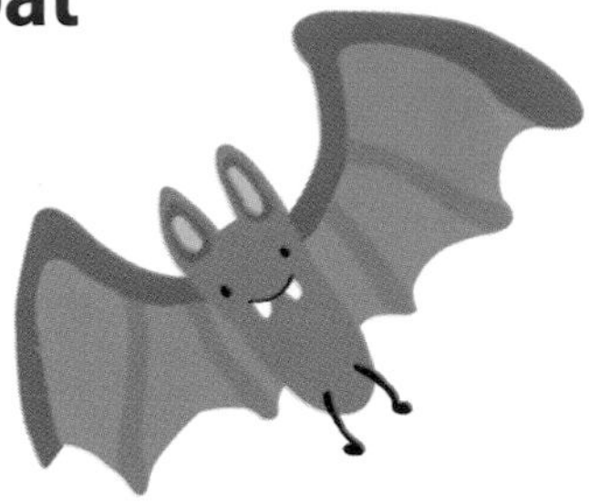

khuffāsh خُفَّاش

bath

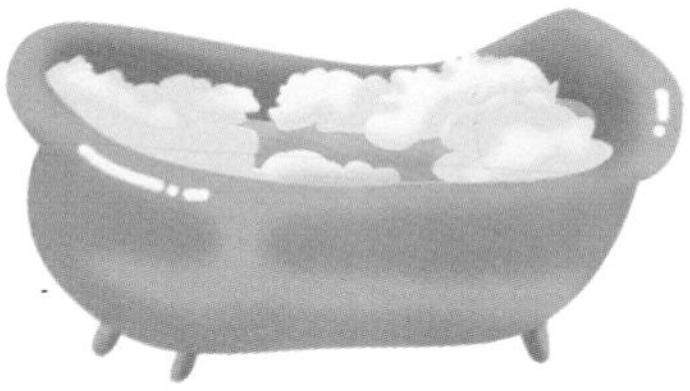

حَوْضُ اِسْتِحْمَام
ḥauḍu istiḥmām

battery

baṭṭāriyyah بَطَّارِيَّة

bay

khalīj خَلِيْج

beach

shāṭi' شَاطِئ

beak

minqār مِنْقَار

bean

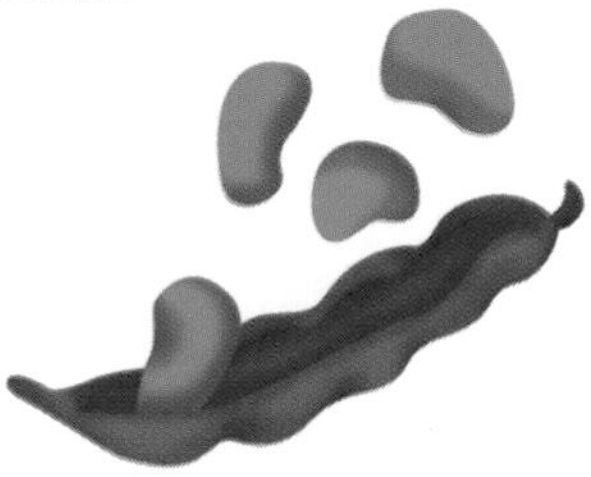

fāṣūliyā فَاصُوْلِيَا

bear

dubb دُبّ

beard

liḥyah لِحْيَة

bed

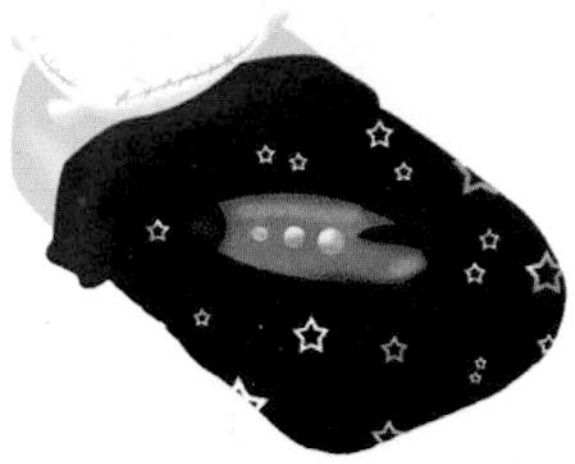

sarīr سَرِيْر

bee

naḥlah نَحْلَة

beetle

khunfusā' خُنْفُسَاء

beetroot

شَمَنْدَر أَحْمَر
shamandar 'aḥmar

bell

jaras جَرَس

belt

ḥizām حِزَام

berry

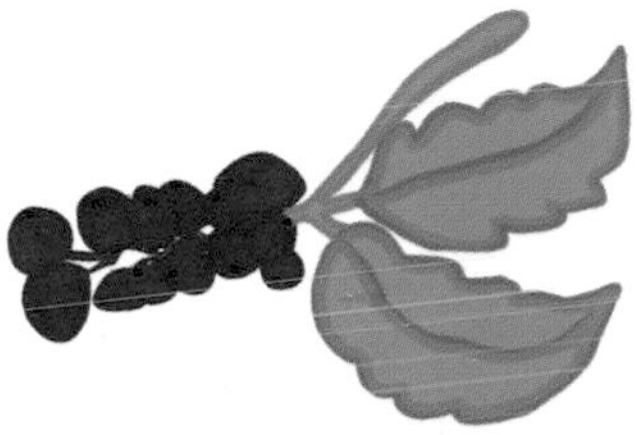

tūt تُوْت

bicycle

darrājah دَرَّاجَة

billiards

bilyārd بِلْيَارْد

bin

سَلَّةُ الْمُهْمَلَات
sallatul muhmalāt

bird

ṭā'ir طَائِر

biscuit

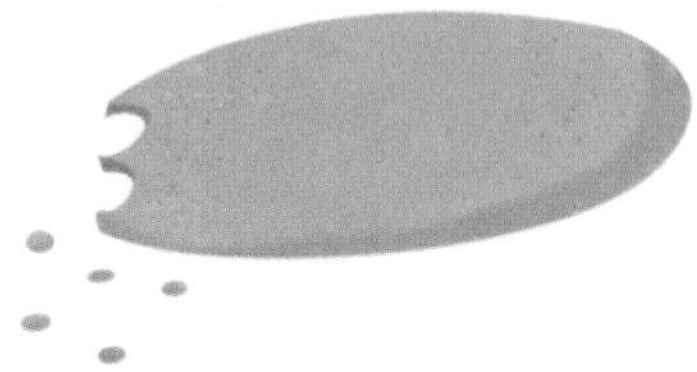

baskawīt بَسْكَوِيْت

black

'aswad أَسْوَد

blackboard

sabbūrah سَبُّورَة

blanket

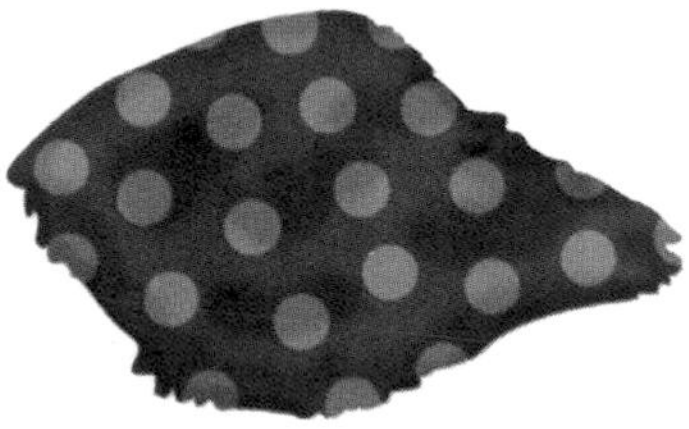

baṭṭāniyyah بَطَّانِيَّة

blizzard

عَاصِفَة ثَلْجِيَّة
'āṣifah thaljiyyah

blood

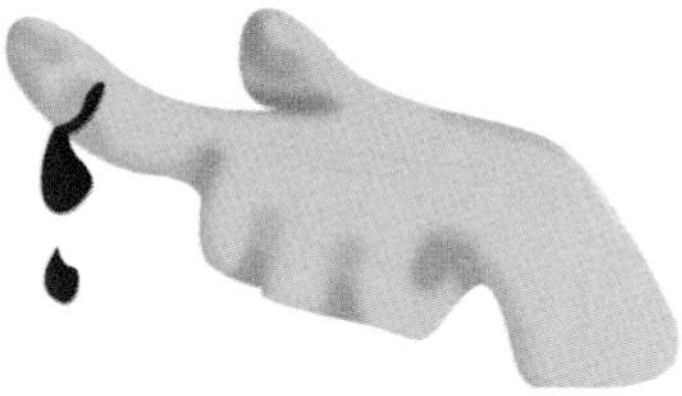

dam دَم

blue

'azraq أَزْرَق

boat

safīnah سَفِيْنَة

body

jism جِسْم

bone

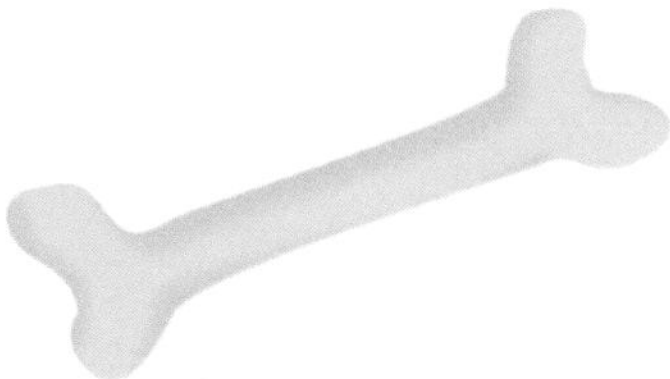

'aẓm عَظْم

book

kitāb كِتَاب

boot

ḥidhā’ حِذَاء

bottle

zujājah زُجَاجَة

bow

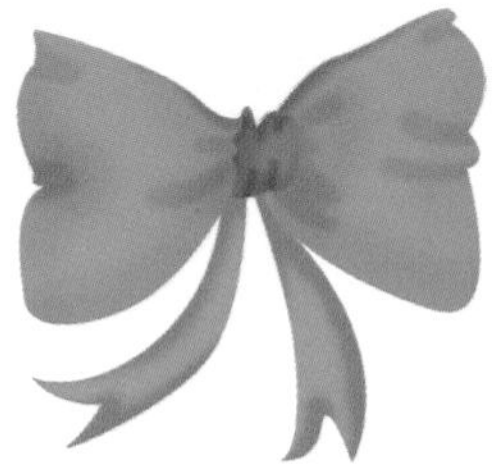

rabṭatul ‘unuq رَبْطَةُ الْعُنُق

bowl

sulṭāniyyah سُلْطَانِيَّة

box

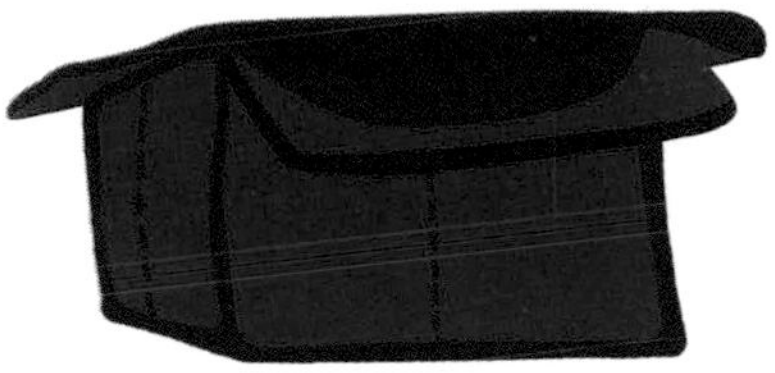

ṣundūq صُنْدُوق

boy

walad وَلَد

bracelet

siwār سِوَار

brain

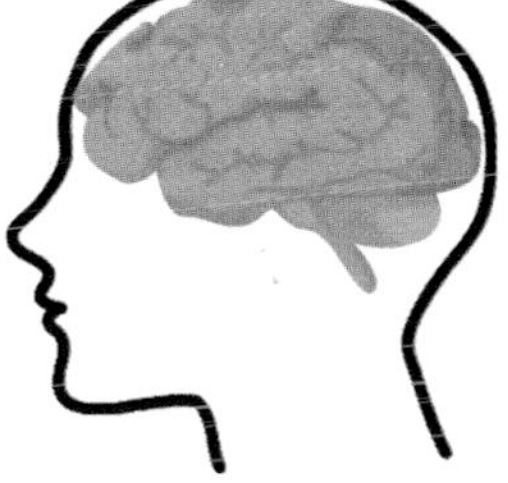

dimāgh دِمَاغ

branch

ghuṣn غُصن

bread

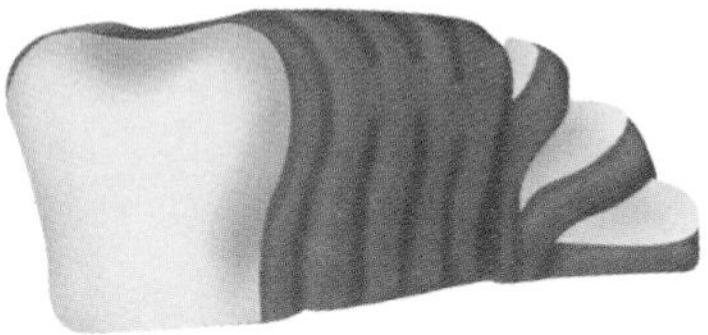

khubz خُبْز

breakfast

faṭūr فَطُور

brick

ṭūb طُوب

a b c d e f g h i j k l m n o p q r s t u v w x y z

bride

ʿarūs عَرُوْس

bridegroom

ʿarīs عَرِيْس

bridge

jisr جِسْر

broom

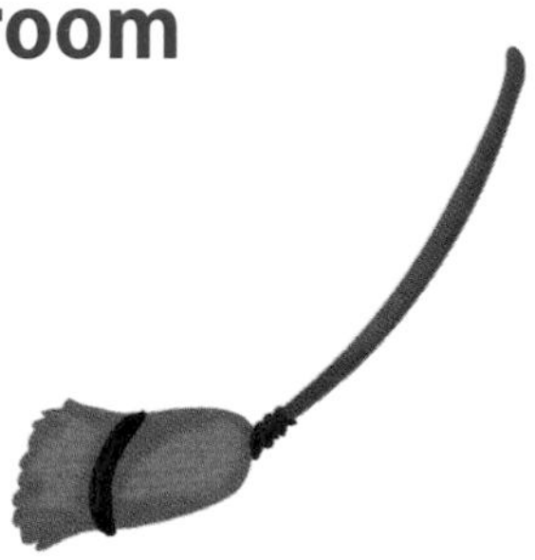

miknasah مِكْنَسَة

brother

ʾakh أَخ

brown

ʾasmar أَسْمَر

brush

furshah فُرْشَة

bubble

fuqqāʿah فُقَّاعَة

bucket

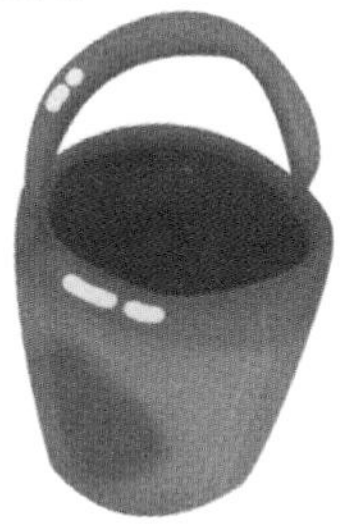

saṭl سَطْل

buffalo

jāmūs جَامُوْس

building

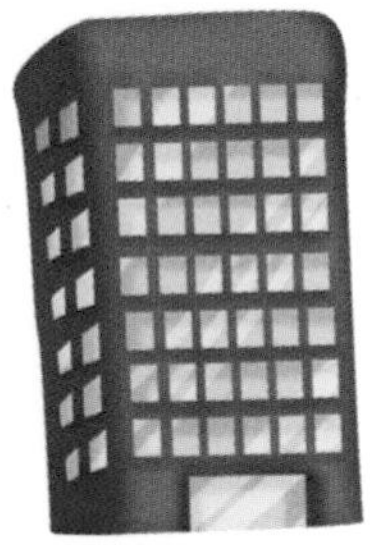

mabna مَبْنًى

bulb

miṣbāḥ مِصْبَاح

bull

thaur ثَوْر

bun

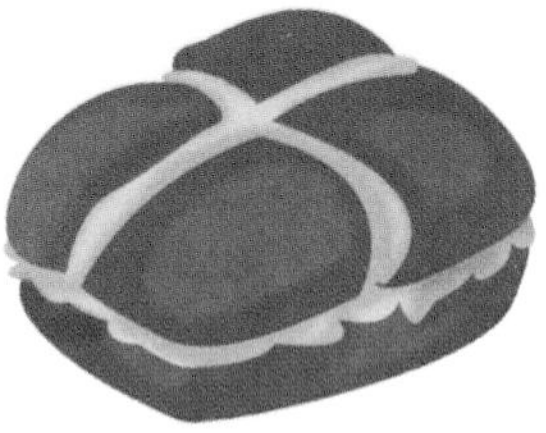

ṣammūn صَمُّون

bunch

bāqah بَاقَة

bundle

ḥuzmah حُزْمَة

bungalow

banghal بَنْغَل

burger

barjar بَرْجَر

bus

ḥāfilah حَافِلَة

bush

shujairah شُجَيْرَة

butcher

jazzār جَزَّار

butter

zubdah زُبْدَة

butterfly

farāshah فَرَاشَة

button

zirr زِرّ

Cc

cabbage

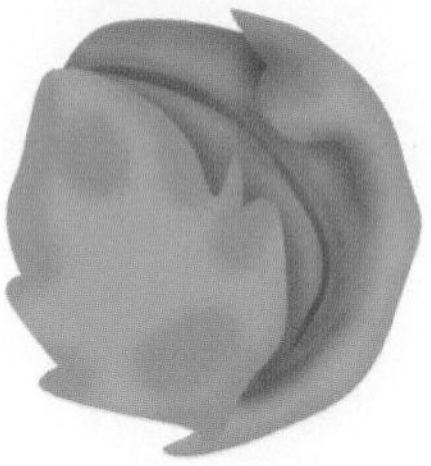

malfūf مَلفُوْف

cabinet

khizānah خِزَانَة

cable

kābil كَابِل

cable car

عَرَبَةُ قِطَار هَوَائِيّ
ʿarabatu qiṭār hawāʾiyy

cactus

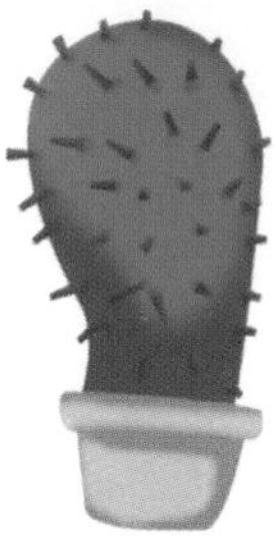

ṣubār صُبَار

cafe

maqha مَقْهى

cage

qafaṣ قَفَص

cake

kaʿkah كَعْكَة

calculator

ʾālah ḥāsibah آلَة حَاسِبَة

calendar

taqwīm تَقْوِيْم

calf

ʿijl عِجْل

camel

jamal جَمَل

camera

kāmīrā كَامِيْرَا

camp

mukhayyam مُخَيَّم

can

ʿulbah عُلْبَة

canal

qanāt قَنَاة

candle

shamʿah شَمْعَة

canoe

alkanw الْكَنْو

canteen

maṭʿam مَطْعَم

cap

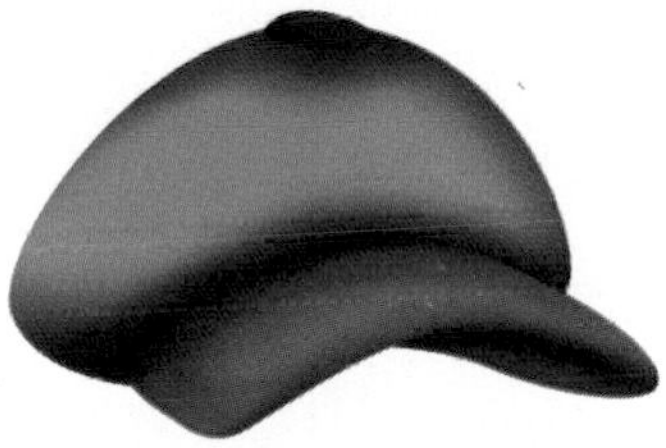

قَلَنْسُوَة/طَاقِيَة
qalansuwah\ṭāqiyah

captain

rubbān رُبَّان

car

sayyārah سَيَّارَة

caravan

qāfilah قَافِلَة

card

waraqul laʿib وَرَقُ اللَّعِب

carnival

mahrajān مَهْرَجَان

carpenter

najjār نَجَّار

carpet

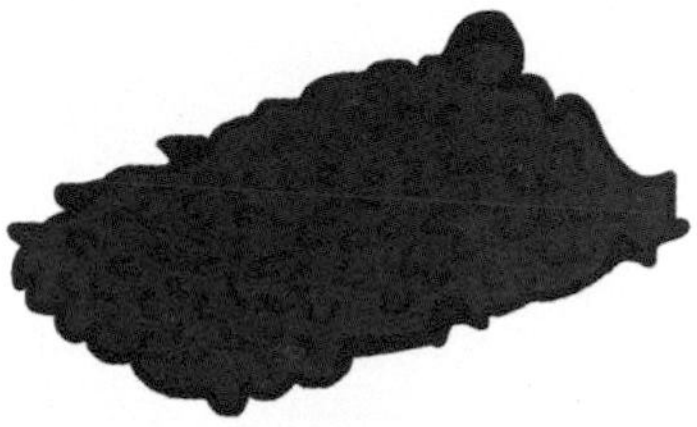

sajjādah سَجَّادَة

carrot

jazar جَزَر

cart

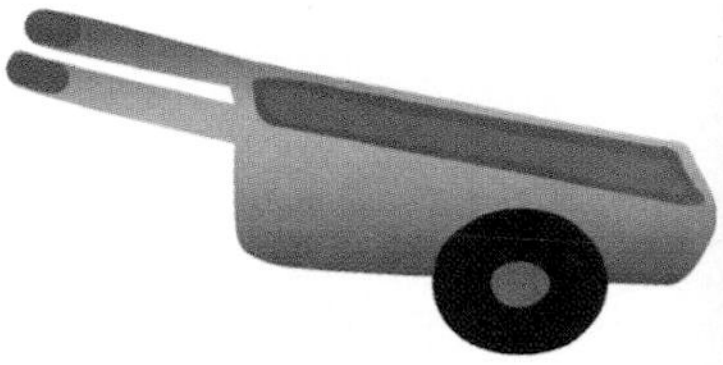

ʿarabah عَرَبَة

cartoon

kārīkātūr كَارِيْكَاتُوْر

cascade

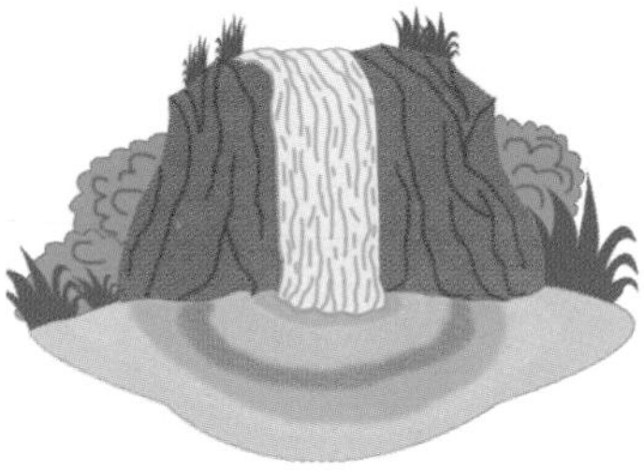

shallāl شَلَّال

castle

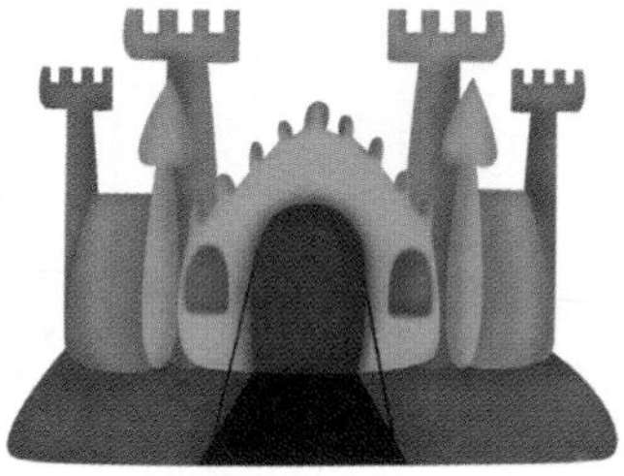

qaṣr قَصْر

cat

qiṭṭ قِطّ

caterpillar

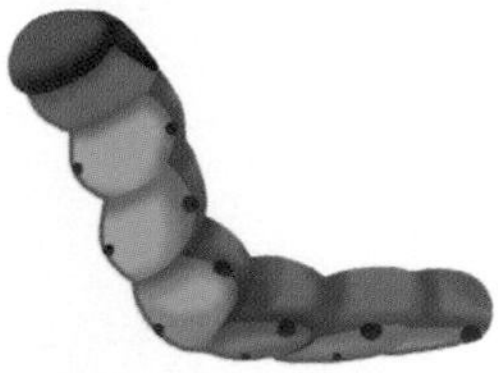

yusrūʿ يُسْرُوْع

cauliflower

qarnabīṭ قَرْنَبِيْط

cave

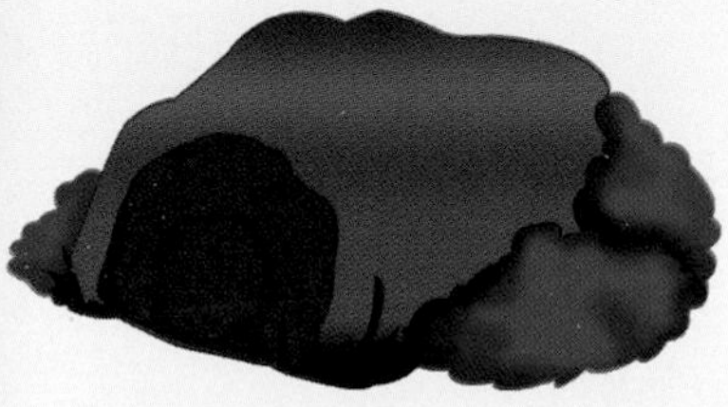

ghār غار

ceiling

saqf سَقْف

centipede

أُمُّ أَرْبَع وَأَرْبَعِيْن
ʾummu ʾarbaʿ wa ʾarbaʿīn

centre
US English **center**

markaz مَرْكَز

cereal

ḥubūb حُبُوْب

chain

silsilah سِلْسِلَة

chair

kursiyy كُرْسِيّ

chalk

ṭabāshīr طَبَاشِيْر

cheek

khadd خَدّ

cheese

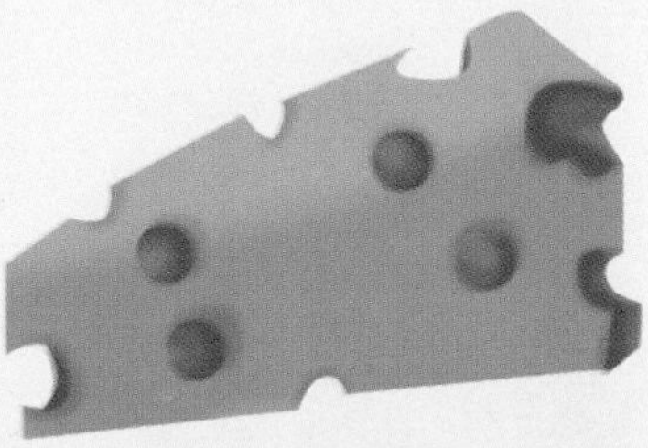

jubn جُبْن

chef

aṭ ṭāhī الطَّاهِي

cherry

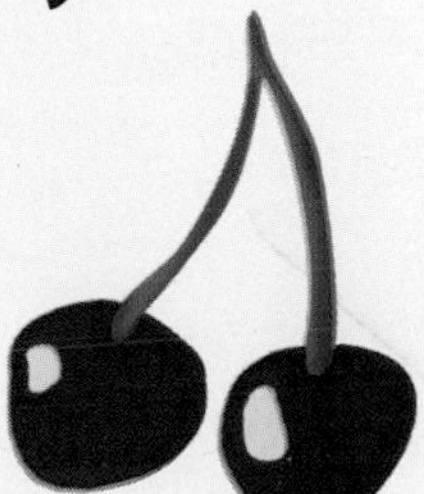

karaz كَرَز

a b c d e f g h i j k l m n o p q r s t u v w x y z

chess

shiṭranj شِطْرَنْج

chest

ṣadr صَدْر

chick

katkūt كَتْكُوْت

chilli
US English **chili**

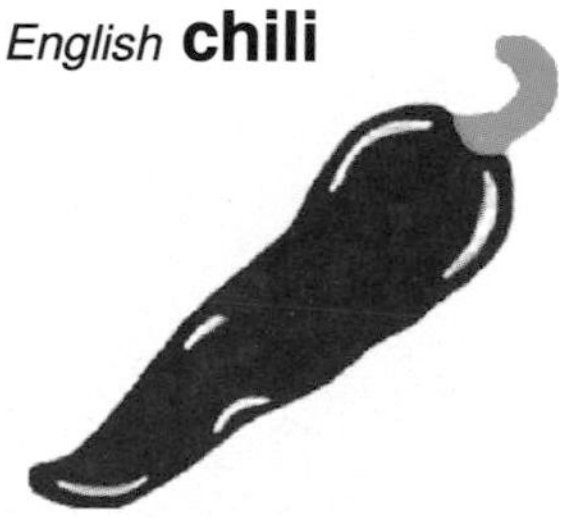

fulful فُلْفُل

chimney

madkhanah مَدْخَنَة

chin

dhaqan ذَقَن

chocolate

شُوْكُوْلَاتَه
shūkūlātah

christmas

عِيْدُ الْمِيْلَاد
ʿīdul mīlād

church

kanīsah كَنِيْسَة

cinema

sīnama سِيْنَمَا

circle

dā'irah دَائِرَة

circus

sīrk سِيْرك

city

madīnah مَدِيْنَة

classroom
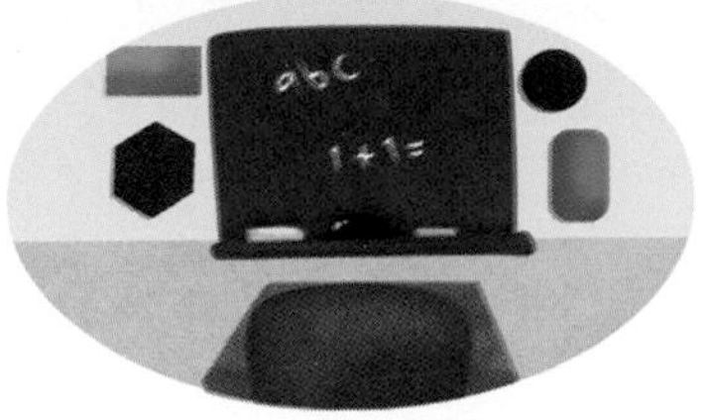

faṣl فَصْل

clinic
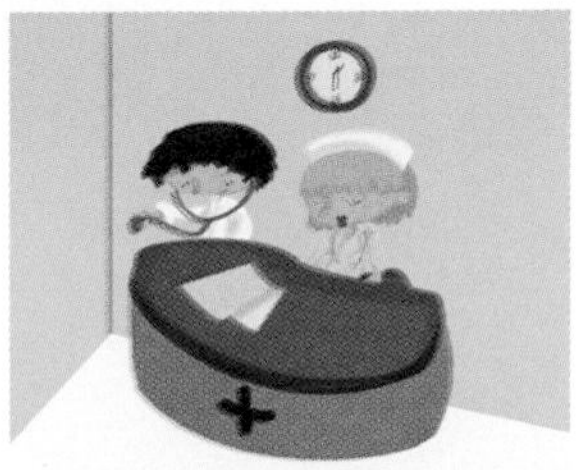

ʿiyādah عِيَادَة

clock

sāʿah سَاعَة

cloth
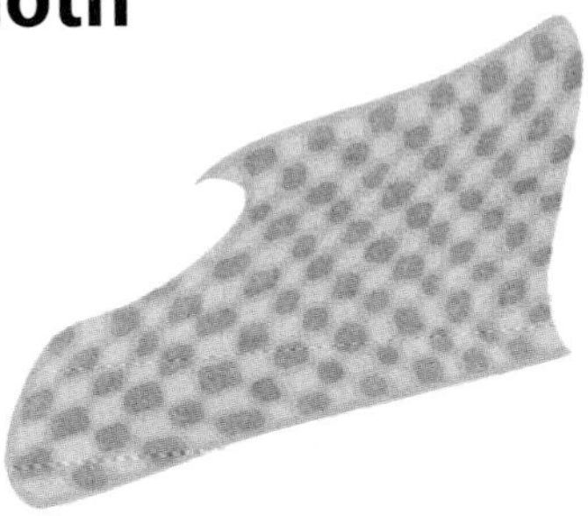

thaub ثَوْب

cloud

saḥābah سَحَابَة

clown

muharrij مُهَرِّج

coal

faḥm فَحْم

coast
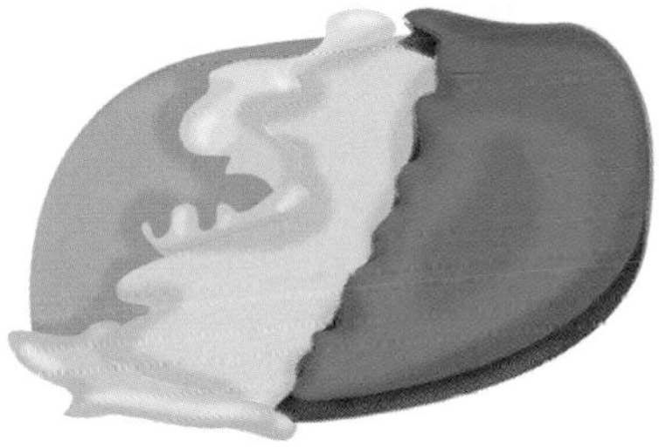

sāḥil سَاحِل

coat

miʿṭaf مِعْطَف

cobra
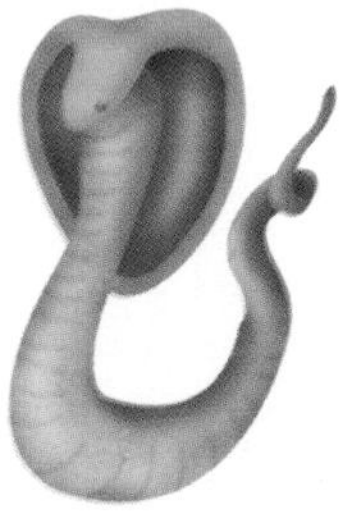

kubrā كُوْبْرَا

cockerel
US English **rooster**

dīk دِيْك

a b **c** d e f g h i j k l m n o p q r s t u v w x y z

cockroach

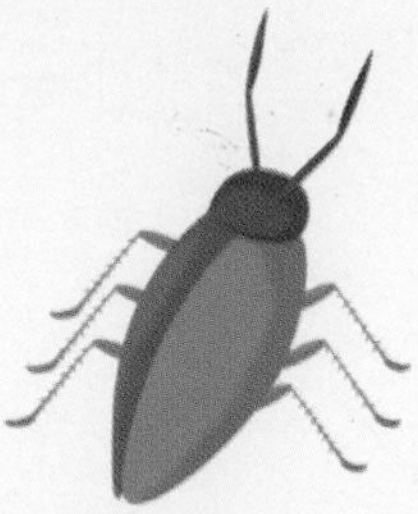

ṣurṣūr صُرْصُور

coconut

nārjīl نَارْجِيْل

coffee

qahwah قَهْوَة

coin

سِكَّة نَقْدِيَّة
sikkah naqdiyyah

colour

US English **color**

laun لَوْن

comb

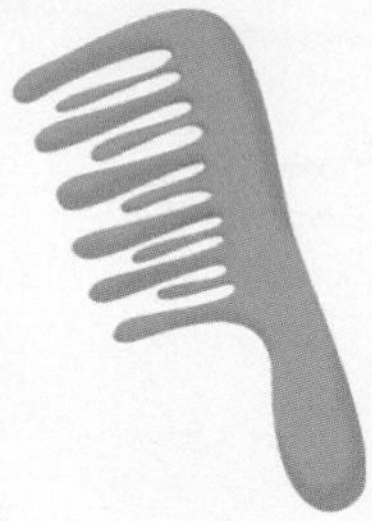

musht مُشْط

comet

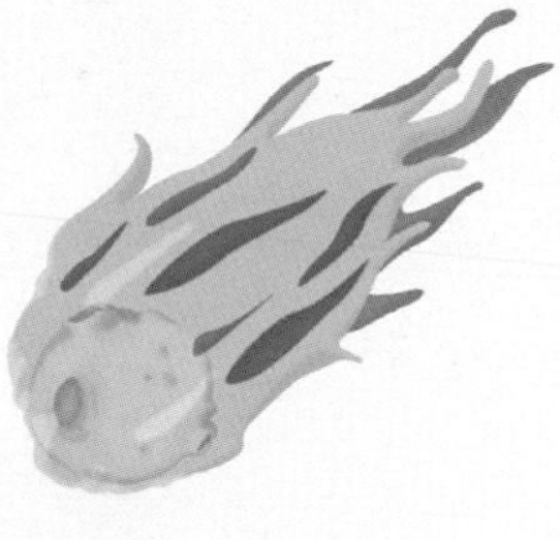

mudhannab مُذَنَّب

compass

būṣlah بُوْصْلَة

computer

ḥāsūb حَاسُوْب

cone

makhrūṭ مَخْرُوْط

container

ʿulbah عُلْبَة

cook

aṭ ṭāhī الطَّاهِي

cookie

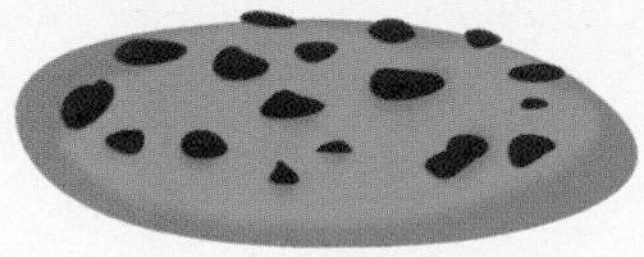

kūkī كُوْكِي

cord

سِلْك كَهْرَبَائِيّ
silk kahrabā'iyy

corn

dhurah ذُرَة

cot

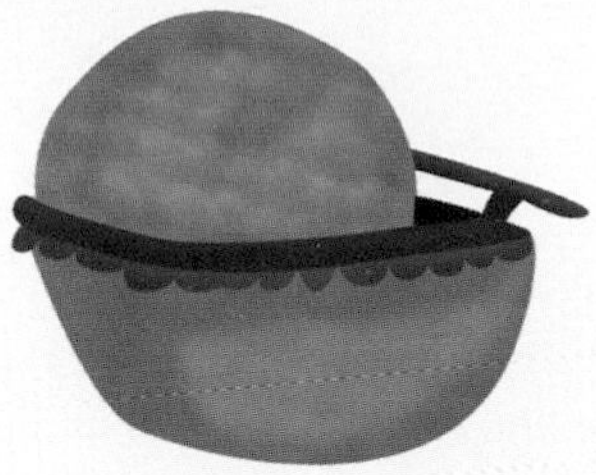

mahd مَهْد

cottage

kūkh كُوْخ

cotton

quṭn قُطْن

country

bilād بِلَاد

couple

zaujān زَوْجَان

court

maḥkamah مَحْكَمَة

cow

baqarah بَقَرَة

crab

saraṭān سَرَطَان

crane

rāfi'ah رَافِعَة

crayon

alkaryūn الْكَرْيُوْن

crocodile

timsāḥ تِمْسَاح

cross

ṣalīb صَلِيْب

crow

ghurāb غُرَاب

crowd

ḥashd حَشْد

crown

tāj تَاج

cube

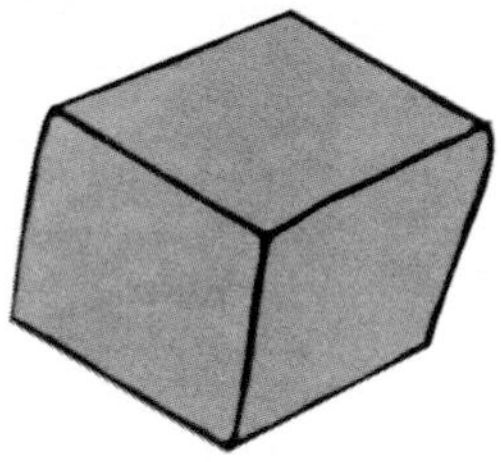

muka‘‘ab مُكَعَّب

cucumber

khiyār خِيَار

cup

finjān فِنْجَان

cupboard

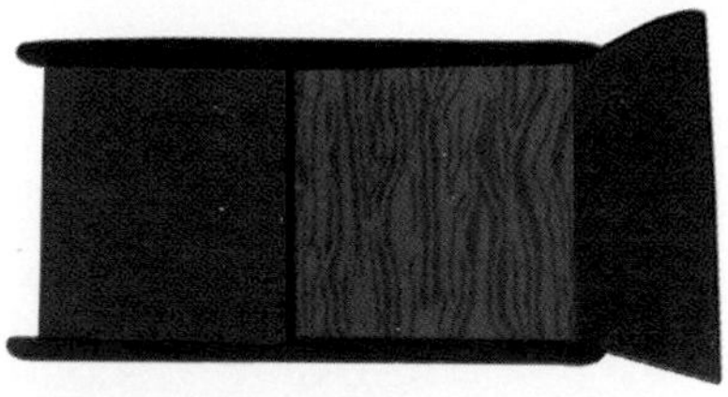

dūlāb دُوْلَاب

curtain

sitārah سِتَارَة

cushion

wisādah وِسَادَة

Dd

dam
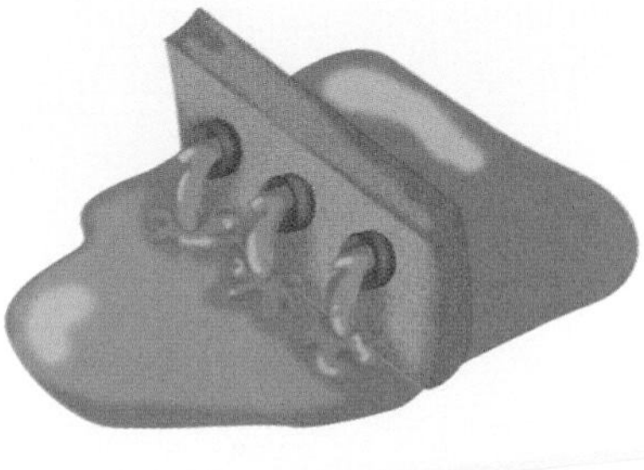

sadd سَدّ

dancer

rāqiṣah رَاقِصَة

dart

sahm سَهْم

data
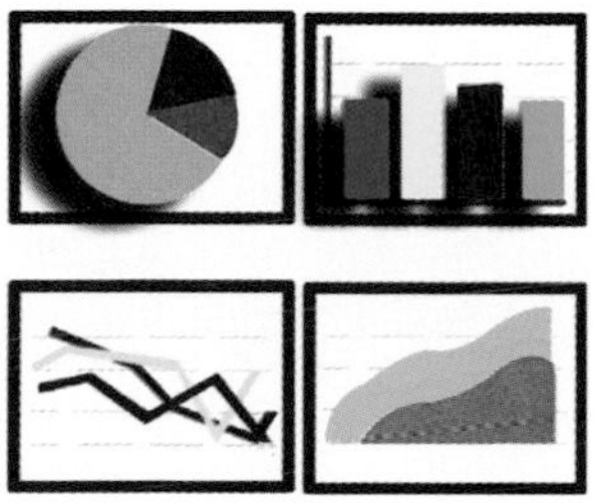

maʿlūmāt مَعْلُومَات

dates

tamr تَمْر

daughter

bint بِنْت

day

nahār نَهَار

deck

شَدَّةُ وَرَقِ اللَّعِب
shaddatu waraqil laʿib

deer

ghazāl غَزَال

den

ʿarīn عَرِيْن

dentist

طَبِيْبُ الْأَسْنَانِ
ṭabībul ʿasnān

a b c d e f g h i j k l m n o p q r s t u v w x y z

desert

ṣaḥrā’ صَحْرَاء

design

taṣmīm تَصْمِيْم

desk

طَاوِلَة/مَكْتَب
ṭāwilah\maktab

dessert

al‘aqabah الْعَقَبَة

detective

būlīs sirriyy بُوْلِيْس سِرِّيّ

diamond

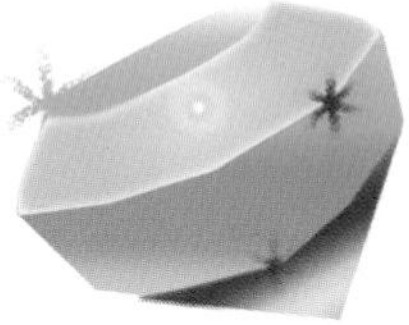

’almās أَلْمَاس

diary

yaumiyyah يَوْمِيَّة

dice

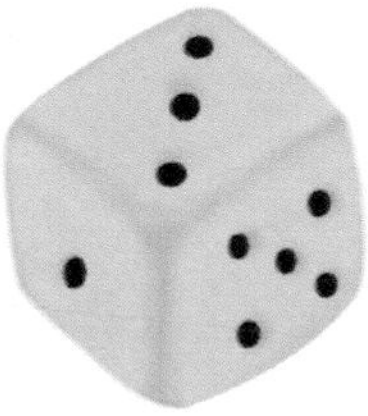

مُكَعَّبُ النَّرْد
muka‘‘abun nard

dictionary

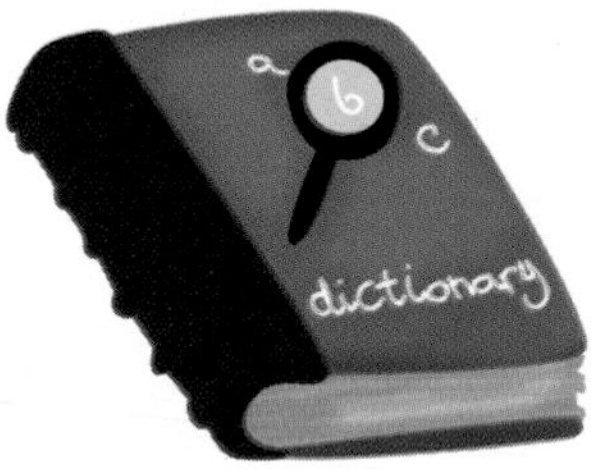

qāmūs قَامُوْس

dinosaur

dainaūṣūr دَيْنوْصُوْر

disc

qurṣ قُرْص

dish

طَبَق/صَحْن
ṭabaq/ṣaḥn

diver

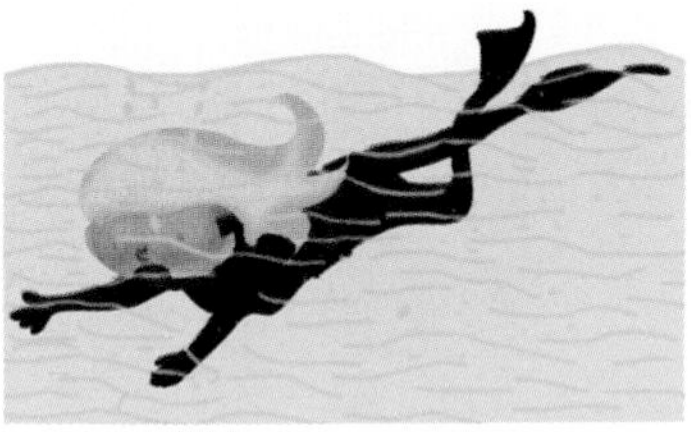

ghawwāṣ غَوَّاص

dock

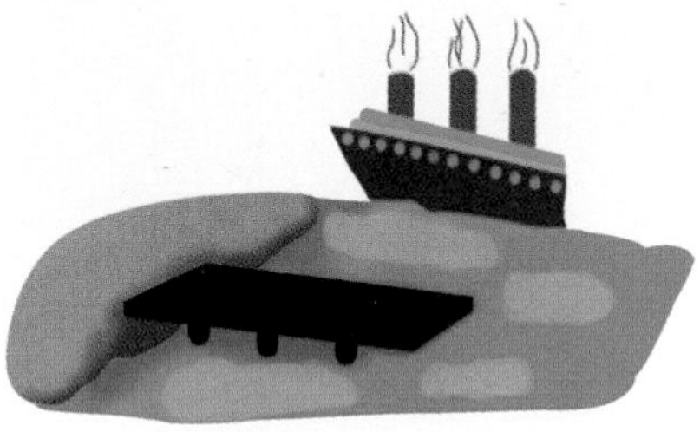

رَصِيْفُ السُّفُن
raṣīfus sufun

doctor

ṭabīb طَبِيْب

dog

kalb كَلْب

doll

dumyah دُمْيَة

dolphin

dulfīn دُلْفِيْن

dome

qubbah قُبَّة

domino

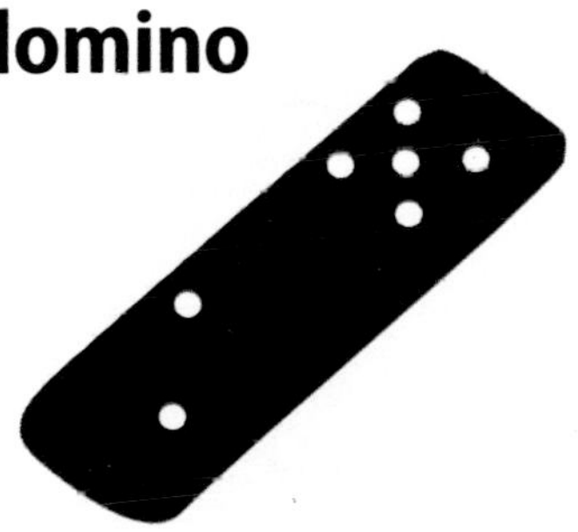

dumīnū دُوْمِيْنُوْ

donkey

ḥimār حِمَار

donut

كَعْكَة مُحَلَّاة
kaʿkah muḥallāt

door

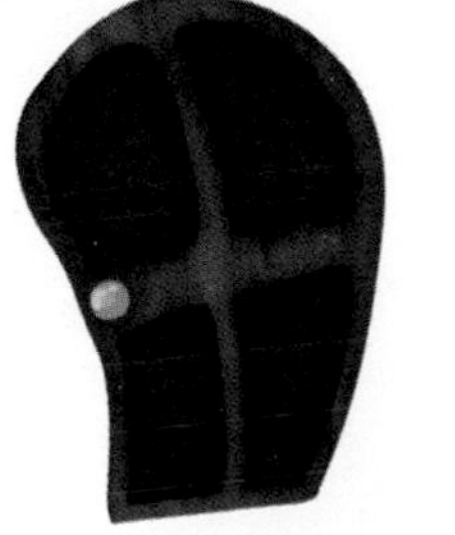

bāb بَاب

dough

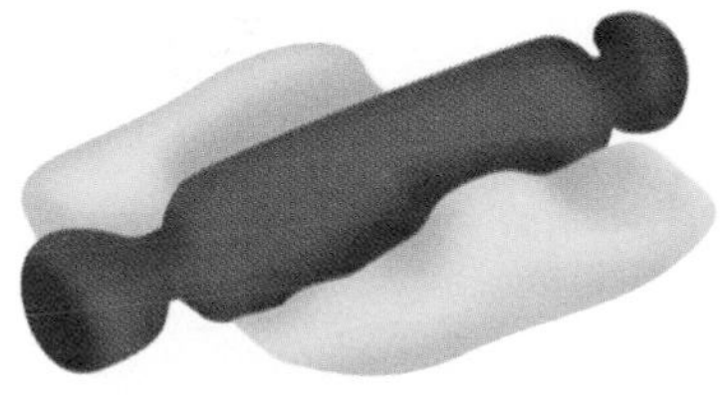

ʿajīn عَجِيْن

dragon

tinnīn تِنِّيْن

drain

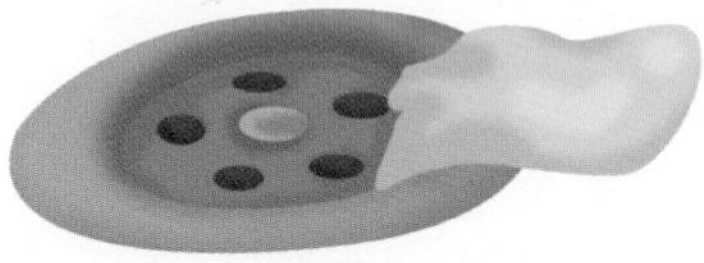

مَصْرِفُ الْمِيَاه/بَالُوْعَة
maṣriful miyāh\bālūʿah

drawer

durj دُرْج

drawing

rasm رَسْم

dream

ḥulm حُلْم

dress

libās لِبَاس

drink

mashrūb مَشْرُوْب

driver

سَائِق/سَوَّاق
sā'iq/sawwāq

drop

qaṭrah قَطْرَة

drought

qaḥṭ قَحْط

drum

ṭabl طَبْل

duck

baṭṭah بَطَّة

dustbin
US English **trash can**

سَلَّةُ الْمُهْمَلَات
sallatul muhmalāt

duvet

liḥāf لِحَاف

dwarf

qazam قَزَم

Ee

eagle

nasr نَسْر

ear

ʾudhn أُذْن

earring

قُرْط/حَلَق
qurṭ/ḥalaq

earth

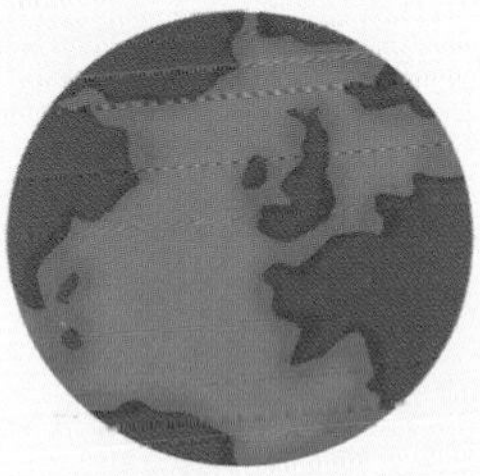

ʾarḍ أَرْض

earthquake

zilzāl زِلْزَال

earthworm

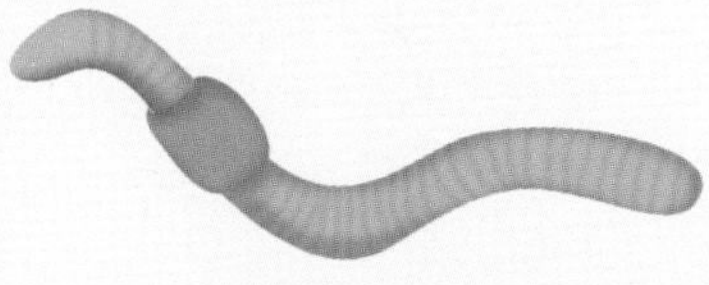

دُودَةُ الْأَرْض
dūdatul ʾarḍ

eclipse

كُسُوف/خُسُوف
kusūf/khusūf

edge

ḥāffah حَافَّة

eel

ʾanqalīs أَنْقَلِيس

egg

baiḍah بَيْضَة

eight

thamāniyah ثَمَانِيَة

elastic

maṭṭaṭah مَطَّاطَة

elbow

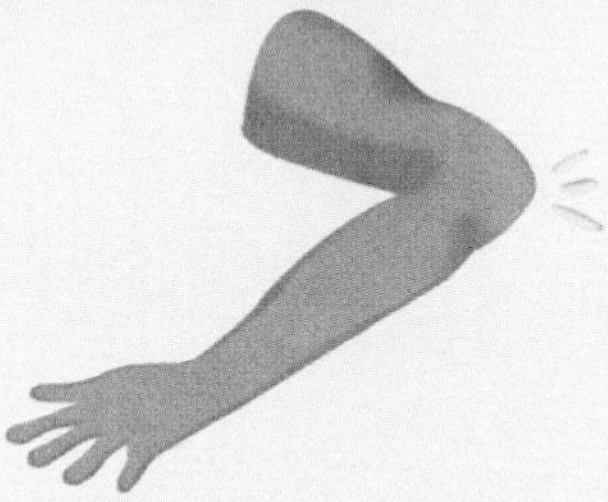

mirfaq مِرْفَق

electrician

kahrabāʾiyy كَهْرَبَائِيّ

electricity

kahrabāʾ كَهْرَبَاء

elephant

fīl فِيْل

elevator

miṣʿad مِصْعَد

elf

ʿifrīt عِفْرِيْت

email

الْبَرِيْدُ الإِلِكْتَرُوْنِي
albarīdul ʾilaktarūnī

embroidery

taṭrīz تَطْرِيز

engine

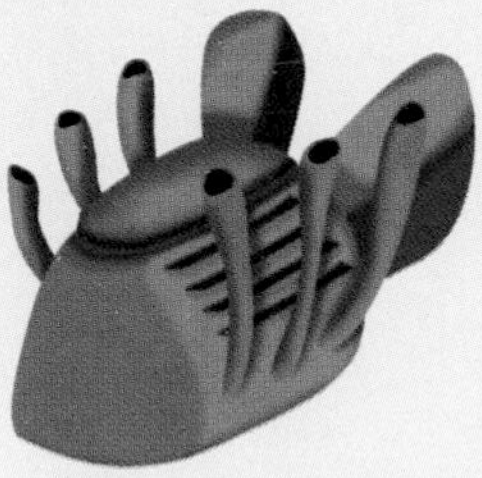

muḥarrik مُحَرِّك

entrance

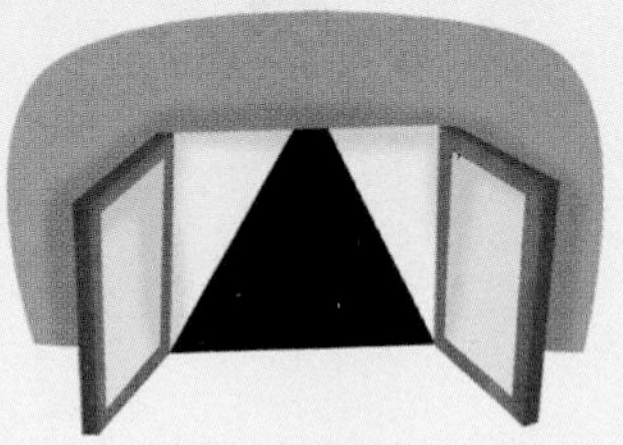

madkhal مَدْخَل

envelope

ẓarf ظَرْف

equator

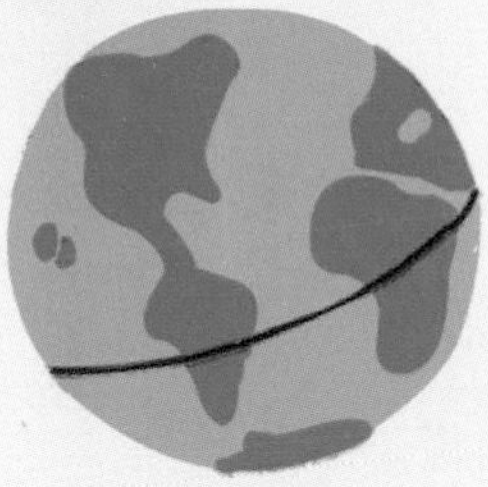

خَطُّ الْاِسْتِوَاء

khaṭṭul istiwā'

equipment

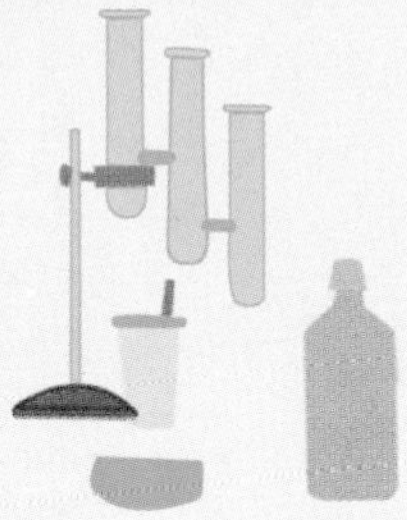

muʿaddāt مُعَدَّات

eraser

mimḥāt مِمْحَاة

escalator

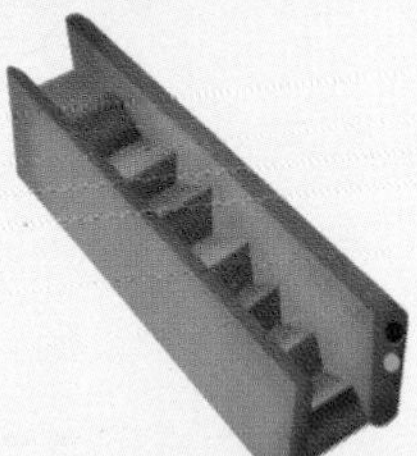

سُلَّم مُتَحَرِّك

sullam mutaḥarrik

eskimo

al'iskīmū الإِسْكِيْمُو

evening

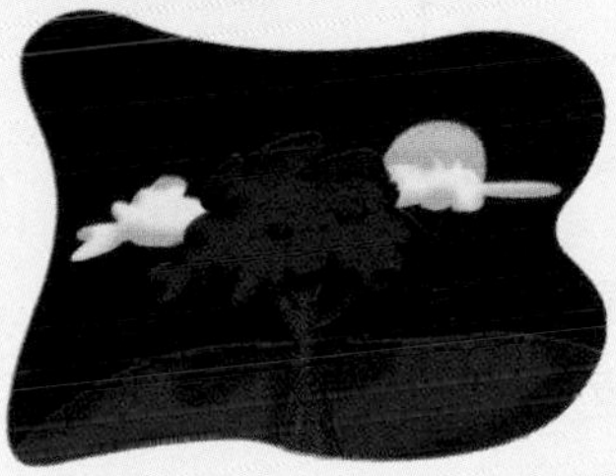

masā' مَسَاء

exhibition

maʿriḍ مَعْرِض

eye

ʿain عَيْن

eyebrow

ḥājib حَاجِب

a b c d e f g h i j k l m n o p q r s t u v w x y z

Ff

fabric

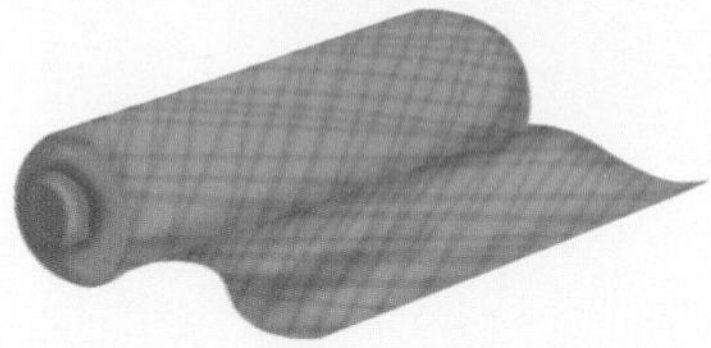

qumāsh قُمَاش

face

wajh وَجْه

factory

maṣnaʿ مَصْنَع

fairy

jinniyyah جِنِّيَّة

family

ʾusrah أُسْرَة

fan

mirwaḥah مِرْوَحَة

farm

mazraʿah مَزْرَعَة

farmer

fallāḥ فَلَّاح

fat

samīn سَمِيْن

father

wālid/ʾab وَالِد/أَب

feather

rīsh رِيْش

female

ʿuntha أُنْثَى

fence

siyāj سِيَاج

ferry

maʿdiyah مَعْدِيَة

field

مَزْرَعَة/حَقْل
mazraʿah/ḥaql

fig

tīn تِيْن

file

milaff مِلَفّ

film

fīlm فِيْلْم

finger

ʾisbaʿ إِصْبَع

fire

nār نَار

fire engine

سَيَّارَةُ الإِطْفَاء
sayyāratul ʾiṭfāʾ

fire fighter

ʾiṭfāʾiyy إِطْفَائِيّ

fireworks

أَلْعَاب نَارِيَة
ʾalʿāb nāriyyah

fish

samak سَمَك

fist

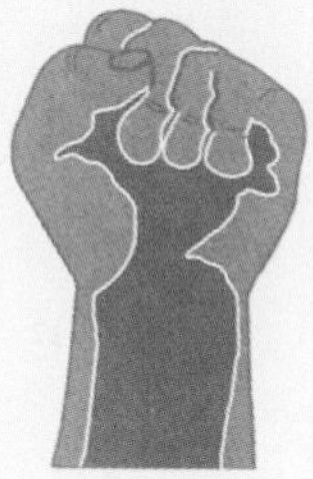

qabḍah قَبْضَة

five

khamsah خَمْسَة

flag

ʿalam/raʾyah عَلَم/رَأْيَة

flame

lahīb لَهِيْب

flamingo

نُحَام/بَشَرُوْش
nuḥām\basharūsh

flask

qārūrah قَارُوْرَة

flock

qatī ʿ قَطِيْع

flood

sail سَيْل

floor

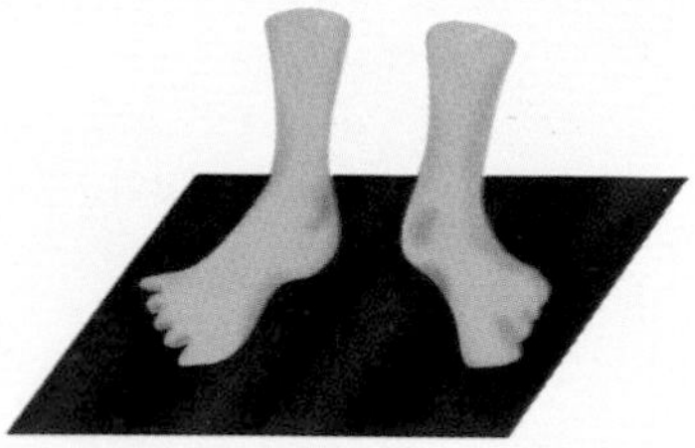

ʾarḍiyyah أَرْضِيَّة

florist

zahhār زَهَّار

flour

daqīq دَقِيْق

flower

zahrah زَهْرَة

flute
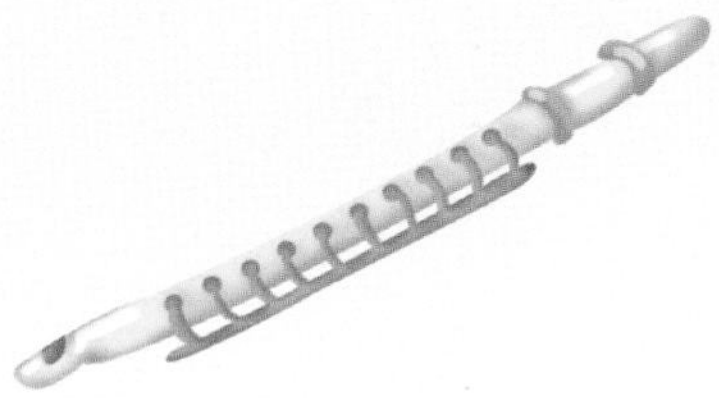

alfulūt الْفُلُوْت

fly

dhubābah ذُبَابَة

foam
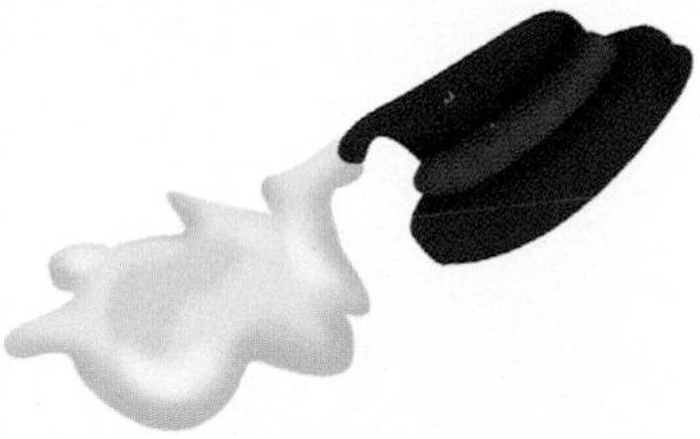

raghwah رَغْوَة

fog

ḍabāb ضَبَاب

foil
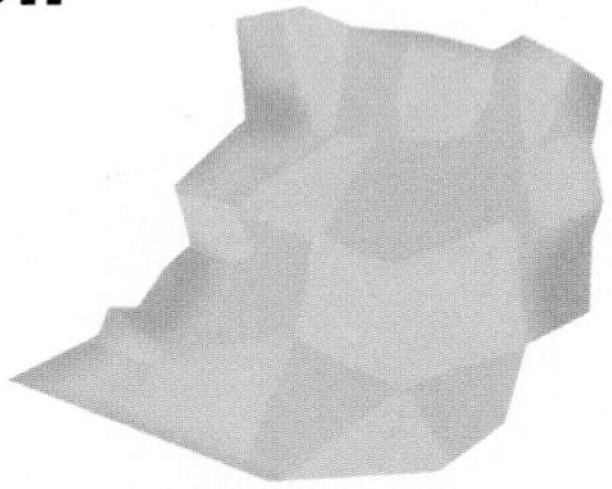

رُقَاقَة مَعْدِنِيَّة
ruqāqah maʿdiniyyah

food
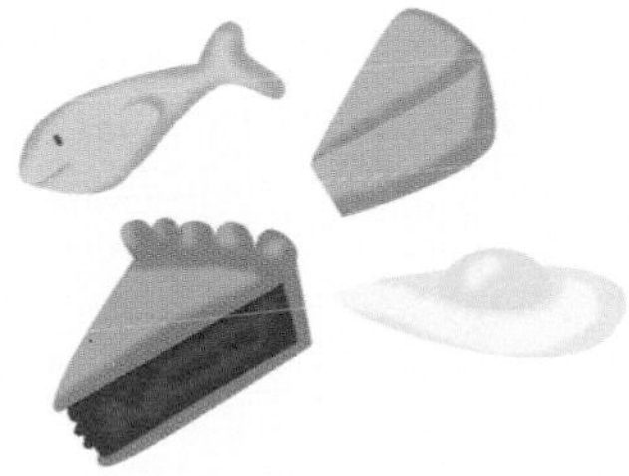

ṭaʿām طَعَام

foot
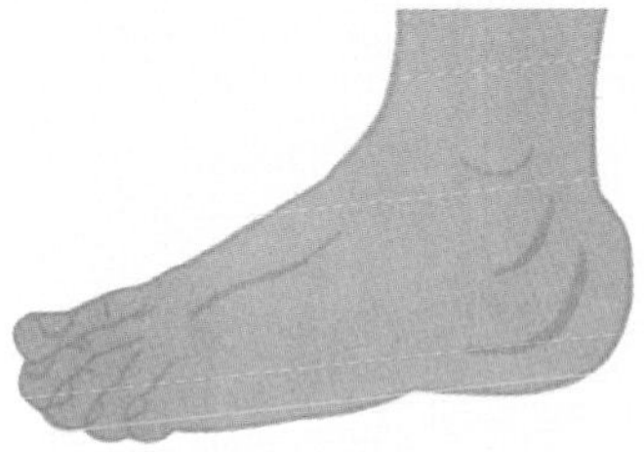

qadam قَدَم

football

kuratul qadam كُرَةُ الْقَدَم

forearm
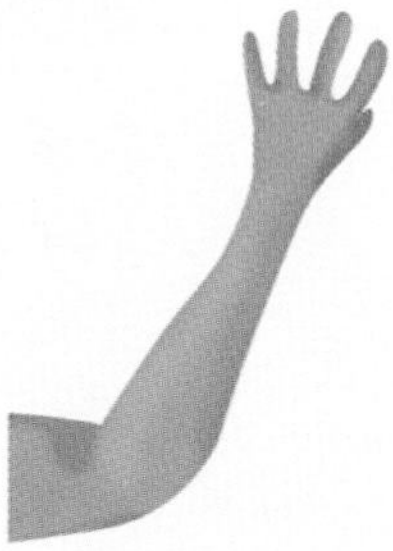

sāʿid سَاعِد

forehead

jabīn جَبِيْن

forest
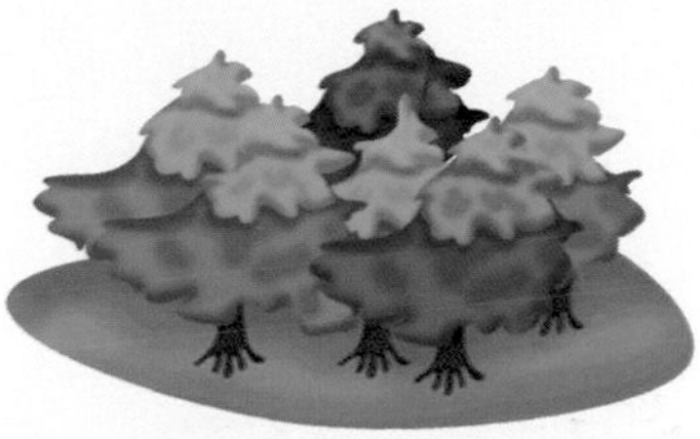

ghābah غَابَة

a b c d e f g h i j k l m n o p q r s t u v w x y z

fork

شَوْكَةُ طَعَام
shaukatu ṭaʿām

fortress

حِصْن/قَلْعَة
ḥiṣn/qalʿah

fountain

nāfūrah نَافُوْرَة

four

ʾarbaʿah أَرْبَعَة

fox

thaʿlab ثَعْلَب

frame

ʾiṭār إِطَار

freezer

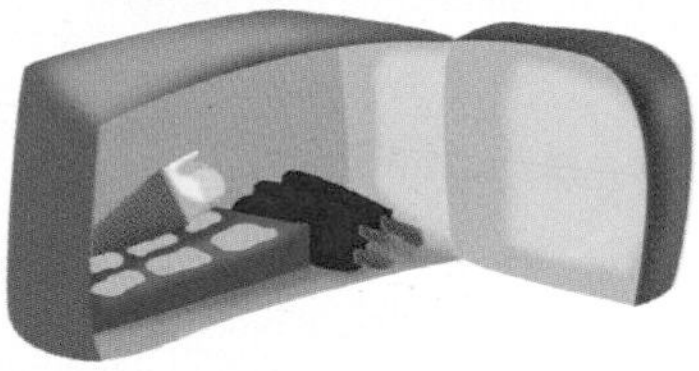

بَرَّاد/فِرِيْزَر
barrād/firīzar

fridge

US English **refrigerator**

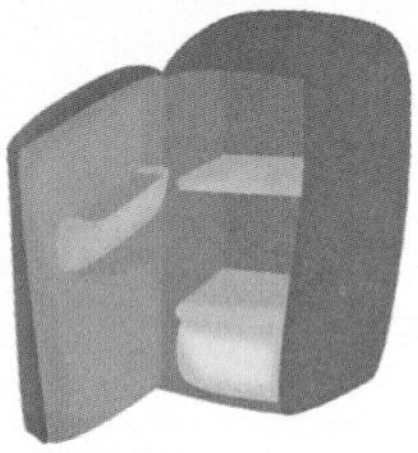

thallājah ثَلَّاجَة

friend

ṣadīq صَدِيْق

frog

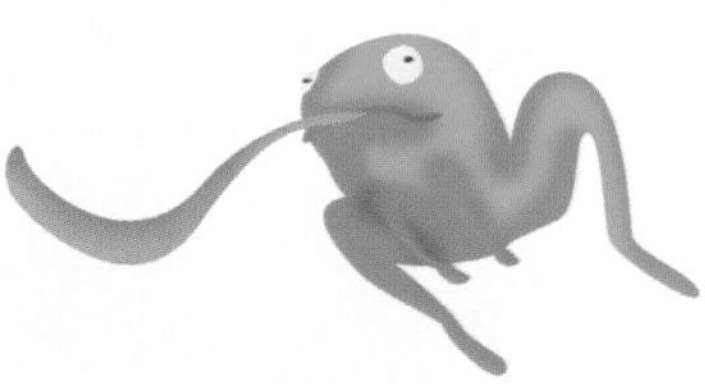

ḍifdaʿ ضِفْدَع

fruit

fawākih فَوَاكِه

fumes

dukhān دُخَان

funnel

qimʿ قِمْع

furnace

furn فُرْن

furniture

ʾathāth أَثَاث

Gg

gadget

ʾadāt أَدَاة

gallery

ṣālatu ʿarḍ صَالَةُ عَرْض

game

luʿbah لُعْبَة

gap

fajwah فَجْوَة

garage

karāj كَرَاج

garbage

qumāmah قُمَامَة

garden

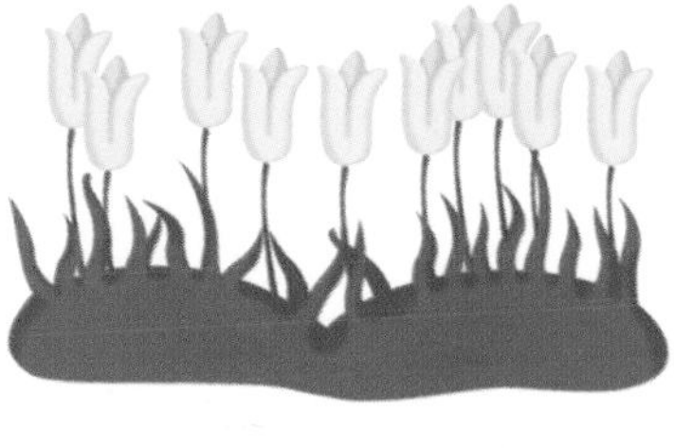

ḥadīqah حَدِيْقَة

garland

ʾiklīl إِكْلِيْل

garlic

thaum ثَوْم

gas

ghāz غَاز

gate

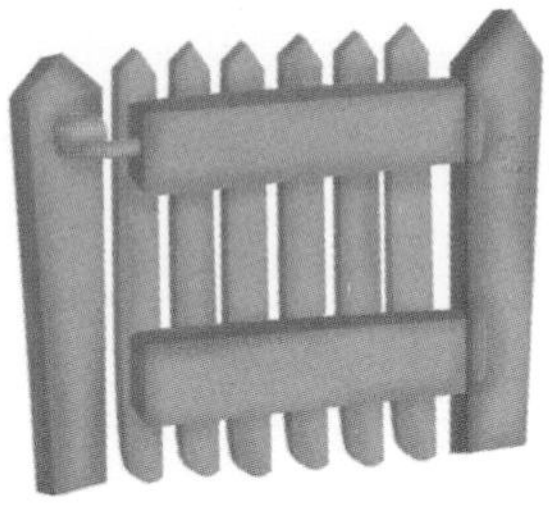

bāb بَاب

gem

jauharah جَوْهَرَة

generator

مُوَلِّد كَهْرَبَائِيّ
muwallid kahrabā'iyy

germ

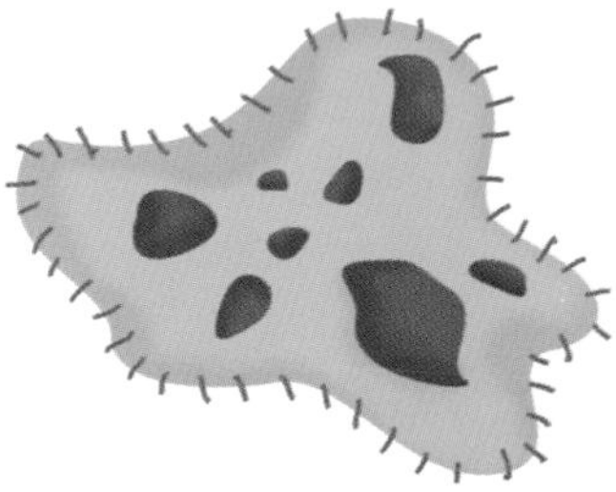

jurthūm جُرْثُوْم

geyser

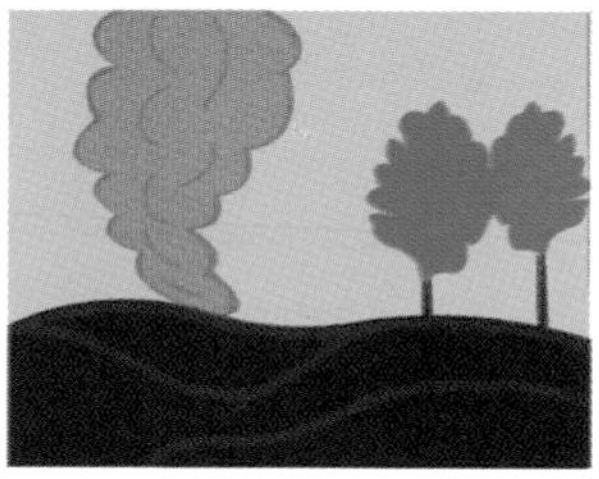

hammah حَمَّة

ghost

shabaḥ شَبَح

giant

ʿimlāq عِمْلَاق

gift

hadiyyah هَدِيَّة

ginger

zanjabīl زَنْجَبِيْل

giraffe

zarāfah زَرَافَة

girl

bint بِنْت

glacier
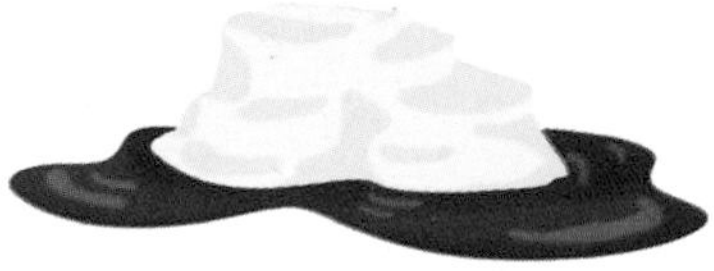

nahrul jalīd نَهْرُ الْجَلِيْد

glass
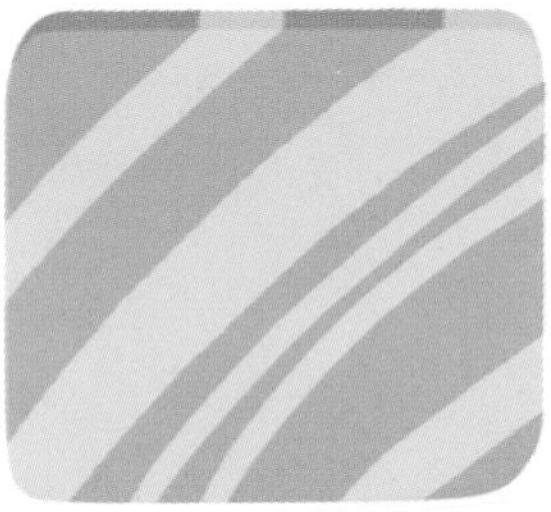

zujāj زُجَاج

glider
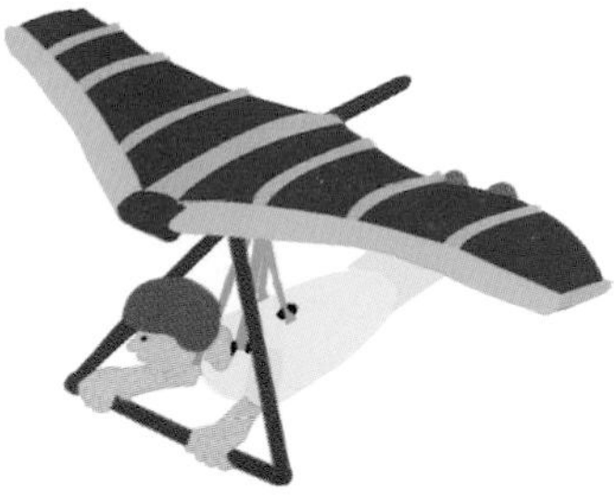

طَائِرَة شِرَاعِيَّة
ṭā'irah shirā'iyyah

globe

kuratul 'arḍ كُرَةُ الْأَرْض

glove

quffāz قُفَّاز

glue

ṣamgh صَمْغ

goal
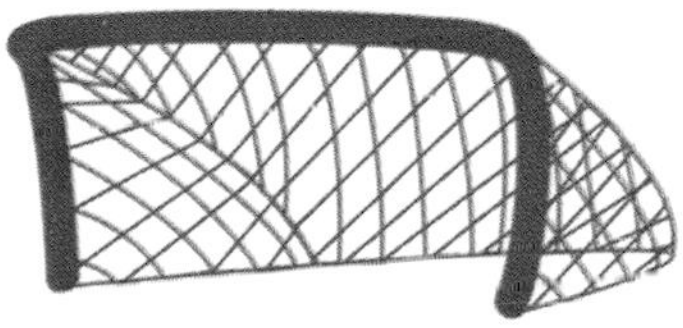

hadaf هَدَف

goat

mā'iz مَاعِز

gold
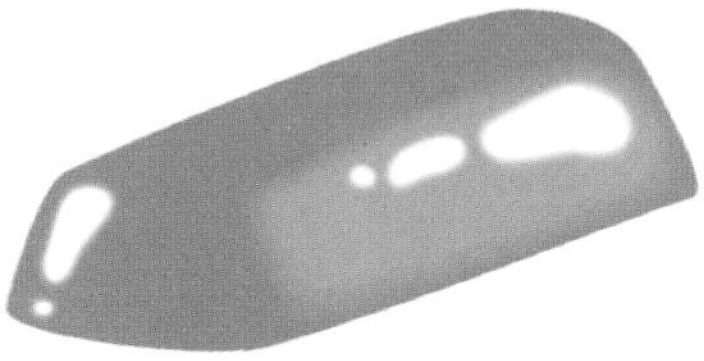

dhahab ذَهَب

golf

jūlf جُوْلْف

goose

وَزَّة/إِوَزَّة
wazzah/'iwazzah

a b c d e f g h i j k l m n o p q r s t u v w x y z

gorilla

ghūrīla غُوْرِيْلَا

grain

ḥubūb حُبُوْب

grandfather

jadd جَدّ

grandmother

jaddah جَدَّة

grape

ʿinab عِنَب

grapefruit

لَيْمُوْن هِنْدِيّ
laimūn hindi

grass

ʿushb عُشْب

grasshopper

jundub جُنْدُب

gravel

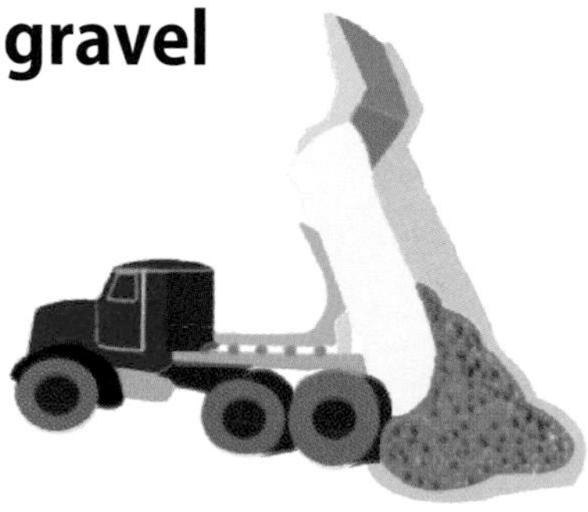

haṣa حَصًى

green

ʾakhḍar أَخْضَر

grey

ramādiyy رَمَادِيّ

grill

mishwāt مِشْوَاة

grocery

biqālah بِقَالَة

ground

maidān مَيْدَان

guard

ḥāris حَارِس

guava

jawāfah جَوَافَة

guide

murshid مُرْشِد

guitar

qīthārah قِيْثَارَة

gulf

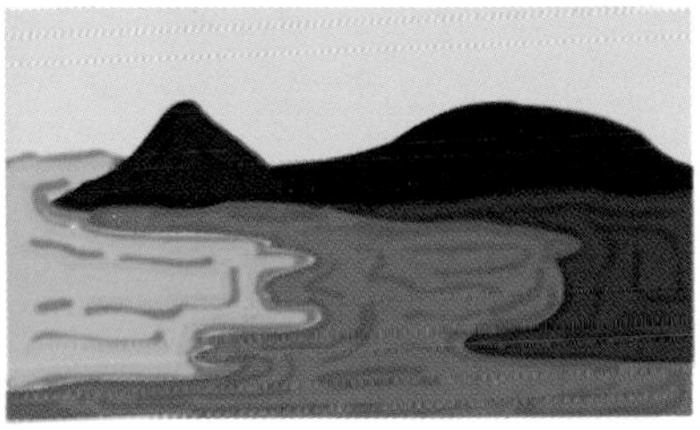

khalīj خَلِيْج

gun

bunduqiyyah بُنْدُقِيَّة

gypsy

ghajariyy غَجَرِيّ

Hh

hair

shaʿr شَعْر

hairbrush

فُرْشَاةُ الشَّعْر
furshātush shaʿr

hairdresser

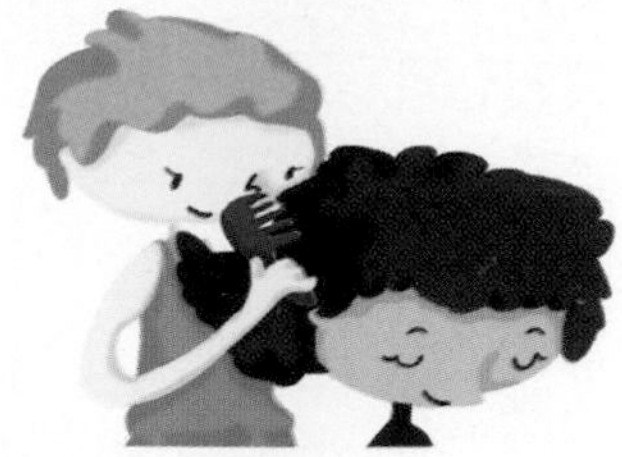

ḥallāq حَلَّاق

half

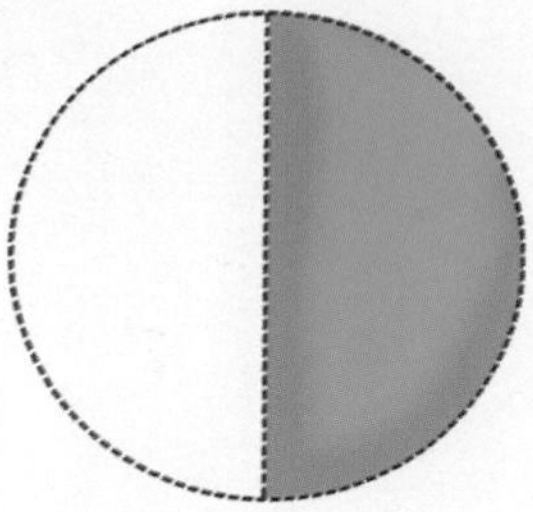

niṣf نِصْف

hall

قَاعَةُ سِيْنَمَا
qāʿatu sīnama

ham

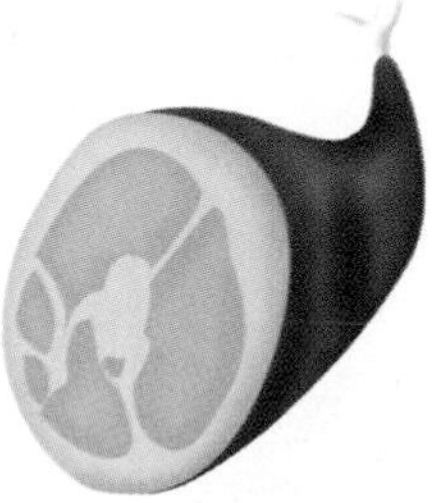

لَحْمُ خِنْزِيْر
laḥmu khinzīr

hammer

miṭraqah مِطْرَقَة

hammock

سَرِيْر مُعَلَّق
sarīr muʿallaq

hand

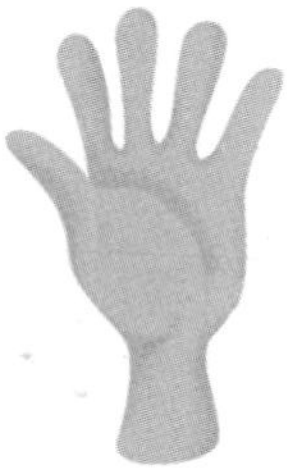

yad يَد

handbag

ḥaqībah حَقِيْبَة

handicraft

صِنَاعَة يَدَوِيَّة
ṣināʿah yadawiyyah

handkerchief

mindīl مِنْدِيْل

handle

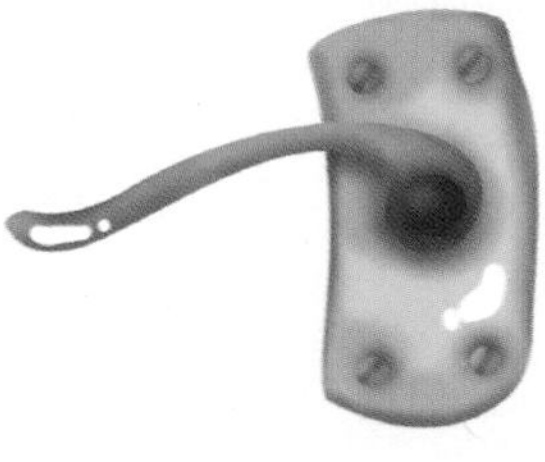

miqbaḍ مِقْبَض

hanger

ʿallāqah عَلَّاقَة

harbour
US English **harbor**

mīnāʾ مِيْنَاء

hare

أَرْنَب وَحْشِيَّة
ʾarnab waḥshiyyah

harvest

ḥaṣād حَصَاد

hat

qubbaʿah قُبَّعَة

hawk

ṣaqr صَقْر

hay

qashsh\tibn قَشّ/تِبْن

head

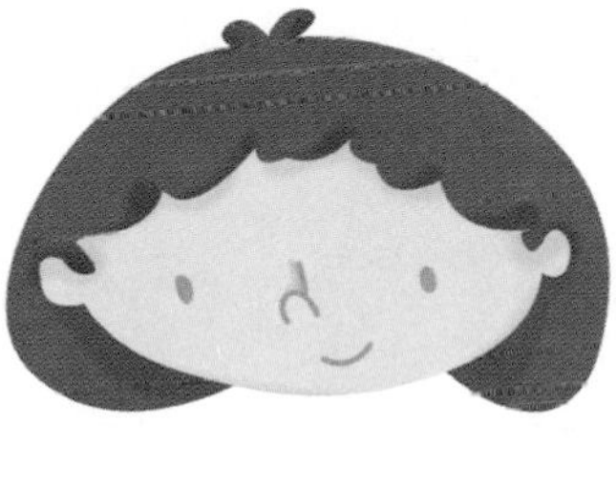

raʾs رَأْس

headphone

سَمَّاعَةُ الرَّأْس
sammāʿatur raʾs

heap

كَوْمَة/رُكَام
kaumah\rukām

heart

qalb قَلْب

heater

سَخَّان/مِدْفَأَة
sakhkhān\midfaʾah

hedge

shujairah شُجَيْرَة

heel

ʿaqib\kaʿb عَقِب/كَعْب

helicopter

طَائِرَة حَوَّامَة
ṭāʾirah ḥawwāmah

helmet

khūdhah خُوْذَة

hen

dajājah دَجَاجَة

herb

ʿushbah عُشْبَة

herd

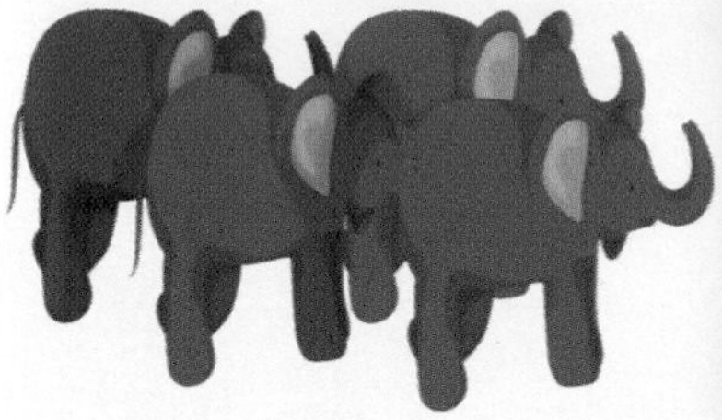

qaṭīʿ قَطِيْع

hermit

nāsik نَاسِك

hill

tall\haḍbah تَلّ/هَضْبَة

hippopotamus

فَرَسُ البَحْر
faras ul baḥr

hive

khaliyatun naḥl خَلِيَةُ النَّحْل

hole

ḥufrah\thuqbah حُفْرَة/ثُقْبَة

honey

shahd\ʿasal شَهْد/عَسَل

hood

قُبَّعَة/قَلَنْسُوَة
qubbaʿah\qalansuwah

hook

kullāb كُلَّاب

horn
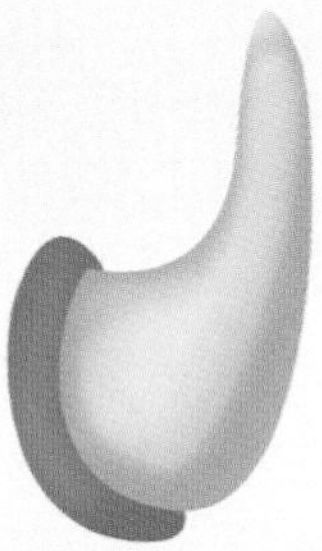
qarn قَرْن

horse

faras\ḥiṣān فَرَس/حِصَان

hose
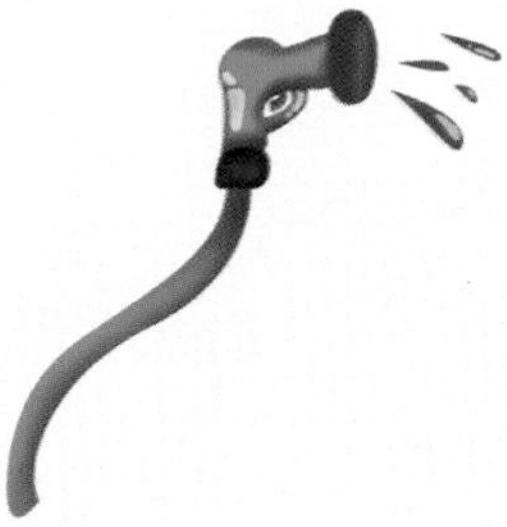
khurṭūmul māʾ خُرْطُومُ الْمَاء

hospital
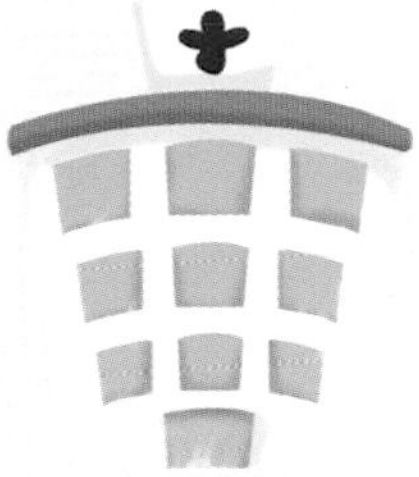
mustashfa مَسْتَشْفَى

hotdog
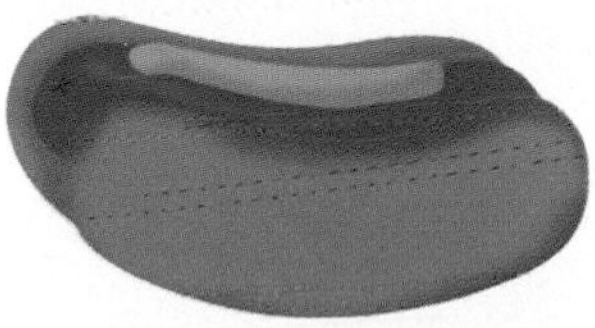
hūt dūj هُوتْ دُوج

hotel

funduq فُنْدُق

hour

sāʿah ramliyyah سَاعَة رَمْلِيَّة

house

dār دَار

human

bashar\ʾinsān بَشَر/إِنْسَان

hunter

ṣayyād صَيَّاد

a b c d e f g h i j k l m n o p q r s t u v w x y z

hurricane

ʾiʿṣār إِعْصَار

husband

zauj زَوْج

hut

kūkh كُوْخ

Ii

ice

jalīd\thalj جَلِيْد/ثَلْج

iceberg

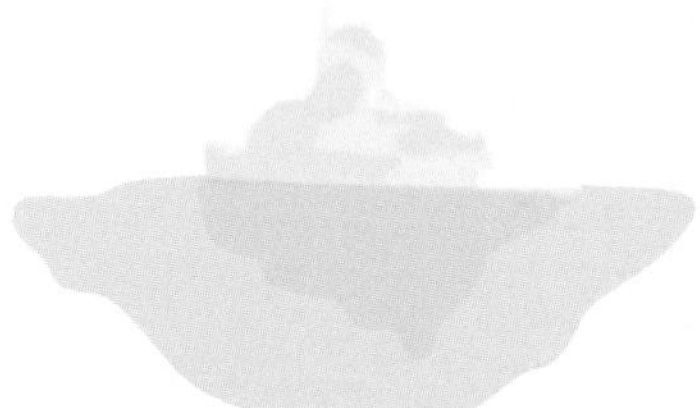

jabal jalīdiyy جَبَل جَلِيْدِيّ

ice cream

بُوْظَة/آيِسْ كِرِيْم
būẓah\ʾāyis kirīm

idol

صَنَم/وَثَن
ṣanam\wathan

igloo

بَيْت جَلِيْدِيّ
bait jalīdiyy

inch

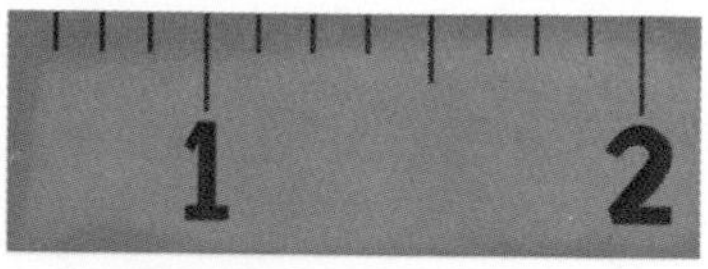

būṣah بُوْصَة

injection

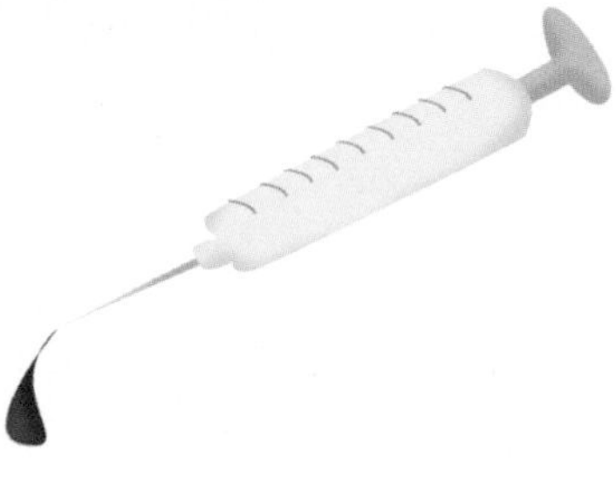

ḥuqnah حُقْنَة

injury

jurḥ جُرْح

ink

ḥibr حِبْر

inn

khān خَان

insect

ḥasharah حَشَرَة

inspector

mufattish مُفَتِّش

instrument

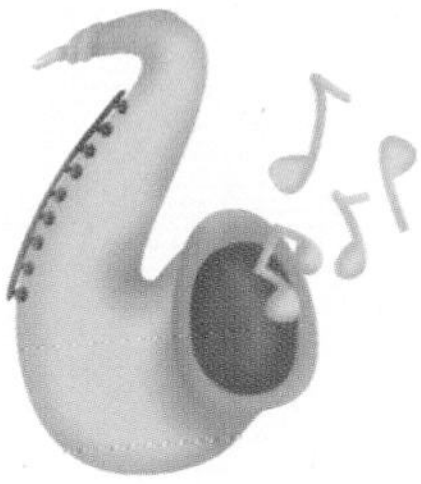

آلَة مُوسِيْقِيَّة
ʾālah mūsīqiyyah

internet

ʾintarnit إِنْتَرنِت

intestine

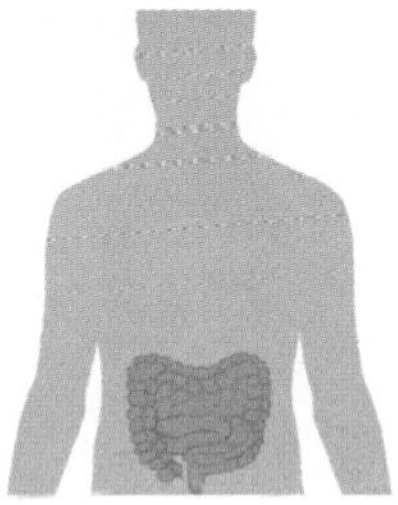

miʿan مِعًى

inventor

mukhtariʿ مُخْتَرِع

invitation

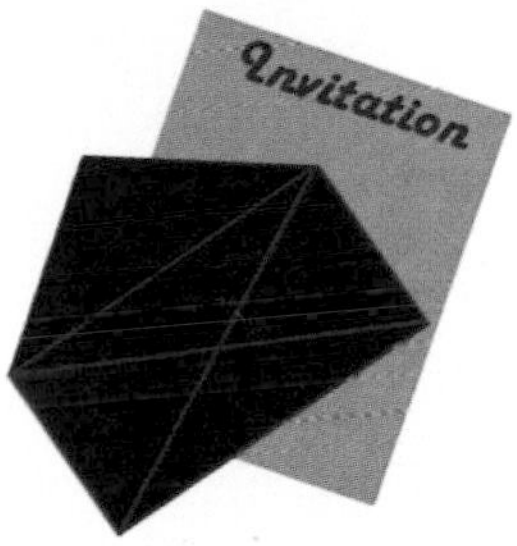

daʿwah دَعْوَة

iron

mikwāt مِكْوَاة

island

jazīrah جَزِيْرَة

ivory

ʿāj عَاج

a b c d e f g h i J k l m n o p q r s t u v w x y z

Jj

jackal

ibnu ʾāwa اِبْنُ آوَى

jacket

جَاكِيْتْ/ سُتْرَة
jākīt\sutrah

jackfruit

jīk furūt جِيْك فُرُوْتْ

jam

murabba مُرَبَّى

jar

marṭabān مَرْطَبَان

javelin

ramyur rumḥi رَمْيُ الرُّمْحِ

jaw

fakk فَكّ

jeans

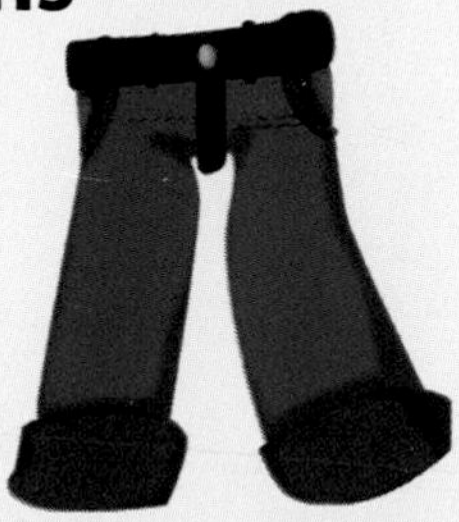

jīnz جِيْنْز

jelly

hulām هُلَام

jetty

حَاجِزُ الْمِيْنَاء
ḥājizul mīnāʾ

jewellery

US English **jewelry**

mujauharāt مُجَوْهَرَات

jigsaw

لُعْبَةُ صُوَر مُقَطَّعَة
luʿbatu ṣuwar muqaṭṭaʿah

jockey

جُوْكِي/فَارِسُ السِّبَاق
jūkī\fārisus sibāq

joker

مُهَرِّج/مَزَّاح
muharrij\mazzāḥ

journey

riḥlah رِحْلَة

jug

ʾibrīq إِبْرِيْق

juggler

mushaʿwidh مُشَعْوِذ

juice

ʿaṣīr عَصِيْر

jungle

دَغَل/أَجَمَة/غَابَة
daghal\ʾajamah\ghābah

jute

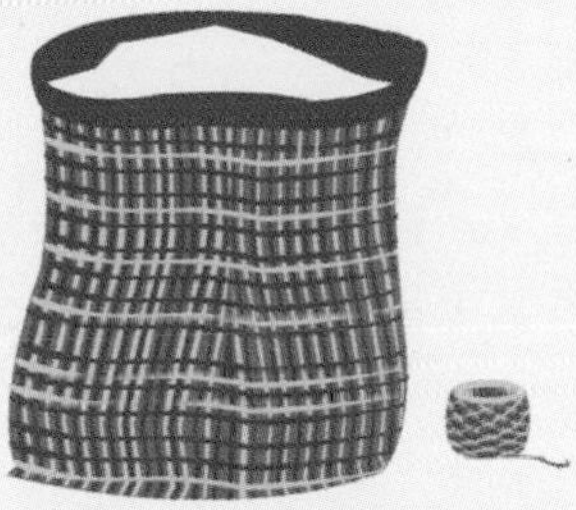

aljūt الْجُوْت

Kk

kangaroo

kanghar كَنْغَر

kennel

wijārul kalb وِجَارُ الْكَلْب

kerb
US English **curb**

حَافَةُ الرَّصِيْف

ḥāfatur raṣīf

kerosene

kīrūsīn كِيْرُوْسِيْن

ketchup

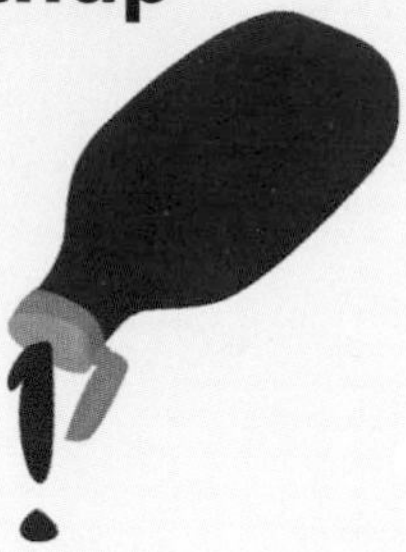

kātshūb كَاتْشُوْب

kettle

غَلَّايَةُ الشَّاي

ghallāyatush shāy

key

miftāḥ مِفْتَاح

keyboard

لَوْحَةُ الْمَفَاتِيْح

lauḥatul mafātīḥ

key ring

حَلَقَةُ الْمَفَاتِيْح

ḥalaqatul mafātīḥ

kidney

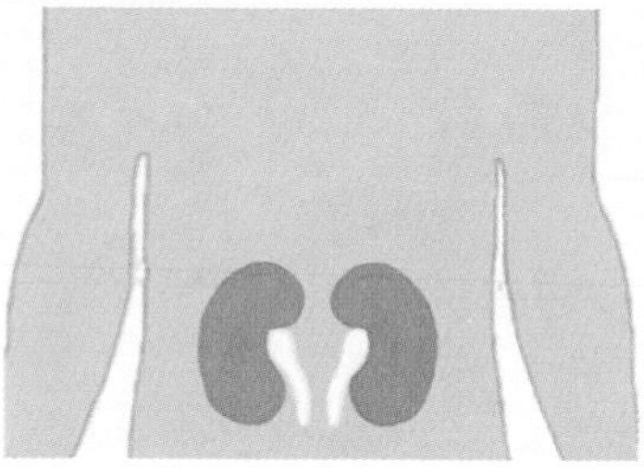

kulyah كُلْيَة

kilogram

kīlūghirām كِيْلُوْغِرَام

king

malik مَلِك

kiosk

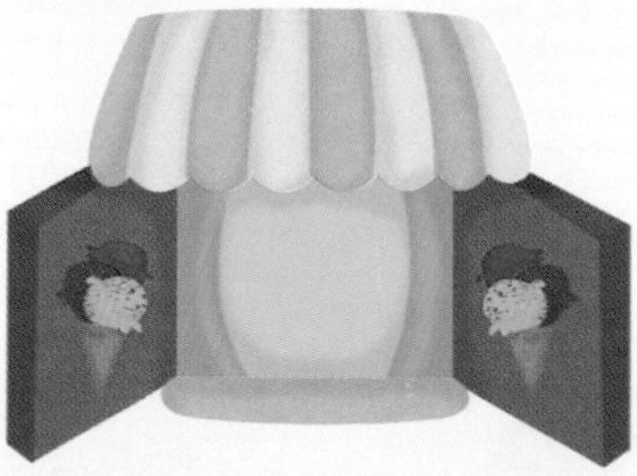

kushk كُشْك

kiss

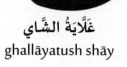

qublah قُبْلَة

kitchen

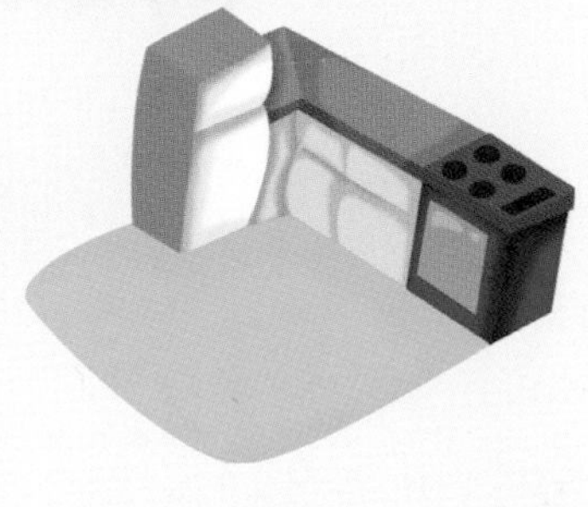

maṭbakh مَطْبَخ

kite

طَائِرَة وَرَقِيَّة
ṭā'irah waraqiyyah

kitten

hurairah هُرَيْرَة

kiwi

kīwī كِيْوِي

knee

rukbah رُكْبَة

knife

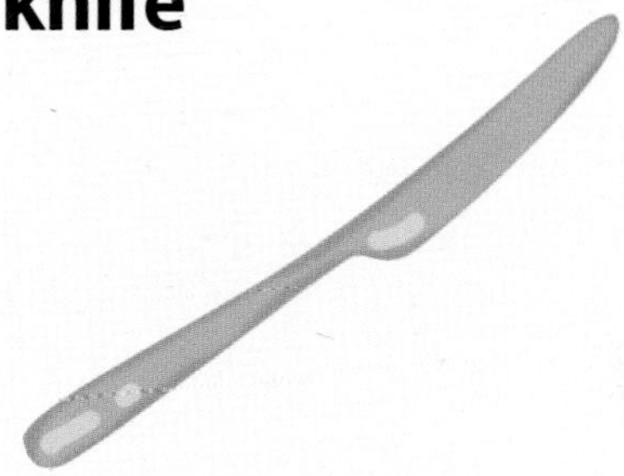

sikkīn سِكِّيْن

knight

fāris فَارِس

knitwear

مَلَابِس صُوْفِيَّة
malābis Ṣūfiyyah

knob

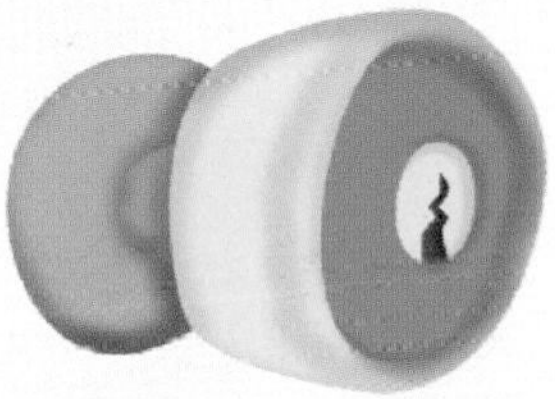

مِقْبَضُ الْبَاب
miqbaḍul bāb

knock

ṭarqah طَرْقَة

knot

ʿuqdah عُقْدَة

knuckle

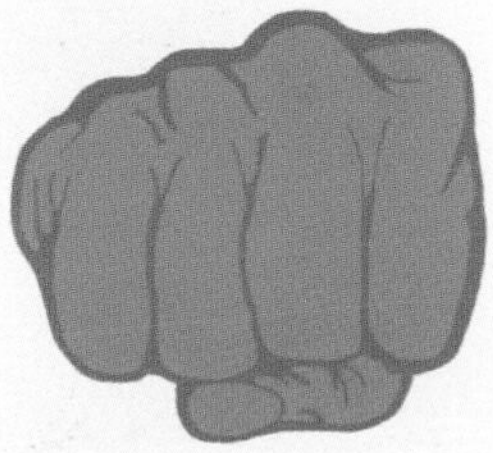

burjumah بُرْجُمَة

Ll

label

biṭāqah بِطَاقَة

laboratory

mukhtabar مُخْتَبَر

lace

رِبَاطُ الْحِذَاء
ribāṭul ḥidhā’

ladder

sullam سُلَّم

lady

sayyidah سَيِّدَة

ladybird

US English **ladybug**

دُعْسُوْقَة
du‘sūqah

lagoon

بُحَيْرَة/هَوْر
buḥairah\haur

lake

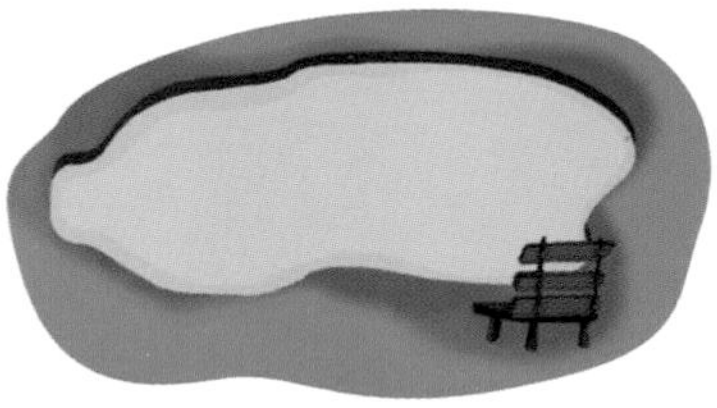

هَوْر/بُحَيْرَة
haur\buḥairah

lamb

حَمَل/خَرُوْف
ḥamal\kharūf

lamp

مِصْبَاح/سِرَاج
miṣbāḥ\sirāj

lamp post

عَمُوْدُ الْكَهْرَبَاءِ
‘amūdul kahrabā’

land

ʾarḍ/ḥaql أَرْض/حَقْل

lane

zuqāq زُقَاق

lantern

fānūs فَانُوْس

laser

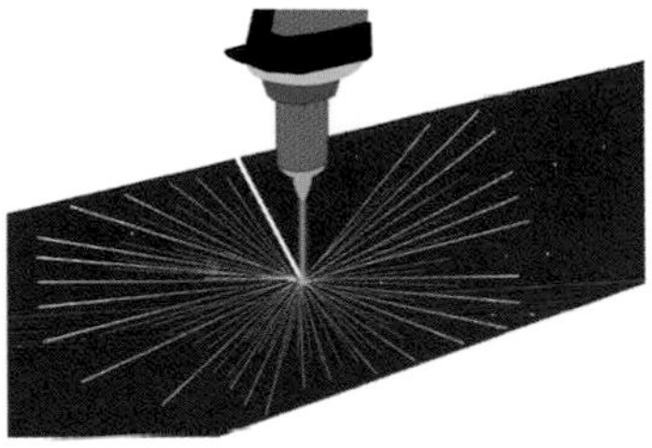

lāzar لَازَر

lasso

wahq وَهْق

latch

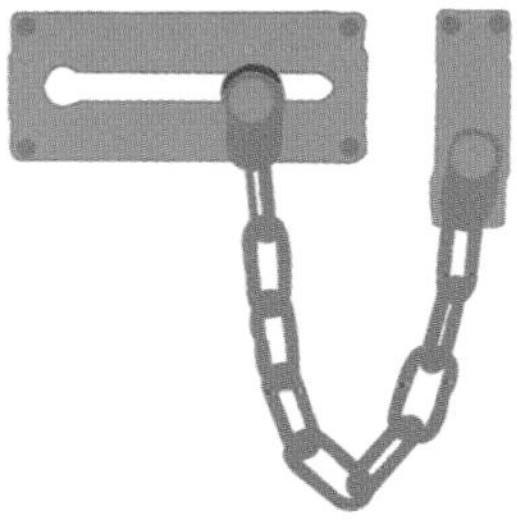

mizlāj مِزلَاج

laundry

ghasīl غَسِيْل

lawn

makhḍarah مَخْضَرَة

lawyer

almuḥāmī الْمُحَامِي

layer

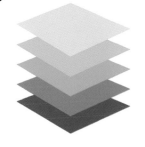

tabaqah طَبَقَة

leaf

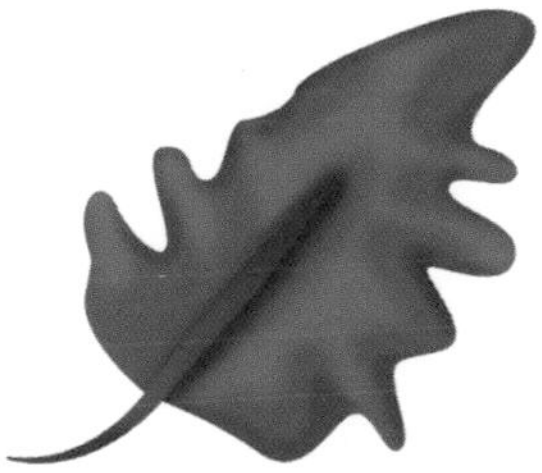

waraq وَرَق

leather

jild جِلْد

leg

rijl رِجْل

lemon

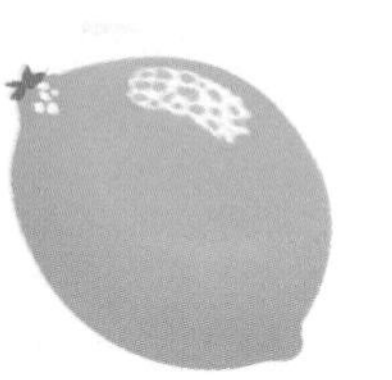

laimūn لَيْمُوْن

lemonade

لَيْمُوْنَادَة
laimūnādah

lens

ʿadasah عَدَسَة

leopard

namir\fahd نَمِر/فَهْد

letter

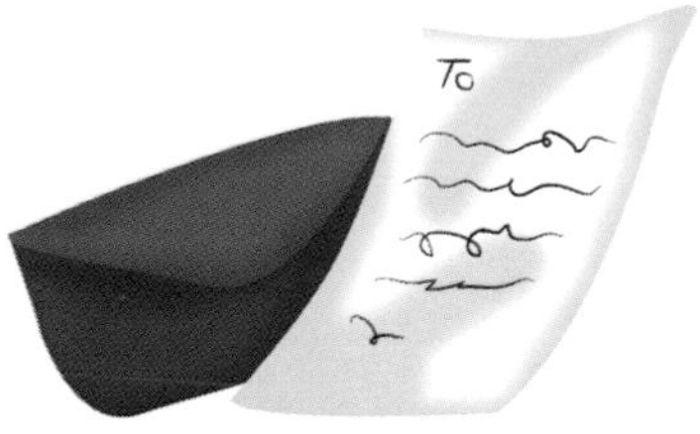

risālah رِسَالَة

letterbox

US English **mailbox**

صُنْدُوْقُ الْبَرِيْد
ṣundūqul barīd

lettuce

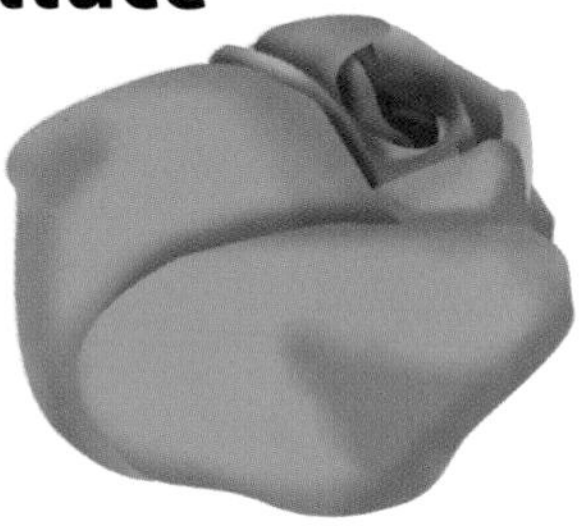

khass خَسّ

library

maktabah مَكْتَبَة

licence

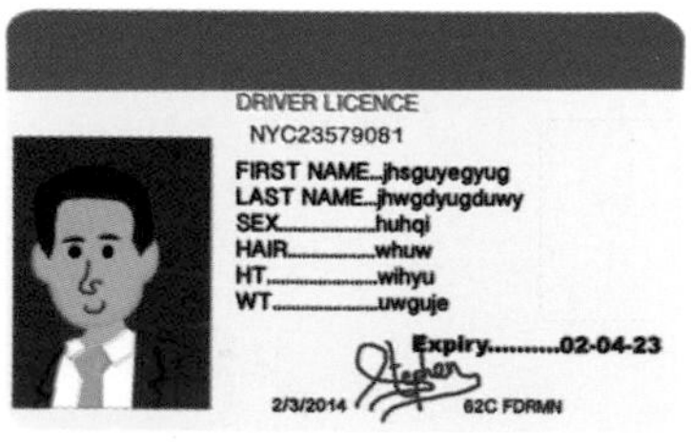

rukhṣah رُخْصَة

lid

ghiṭāʾ غِطَاء

light

ḍauʾ\nūr ضَوْء/نُوْر

lighthouse

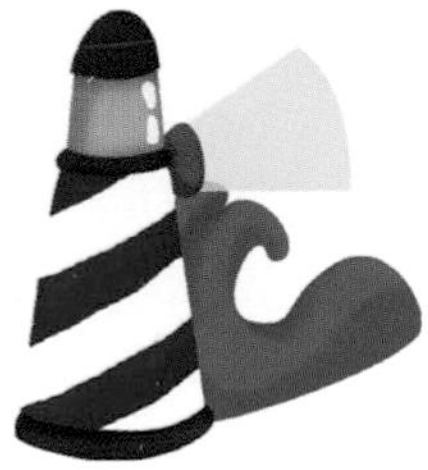

مَنَارَة/فَنَار
manārah\fanār

limb

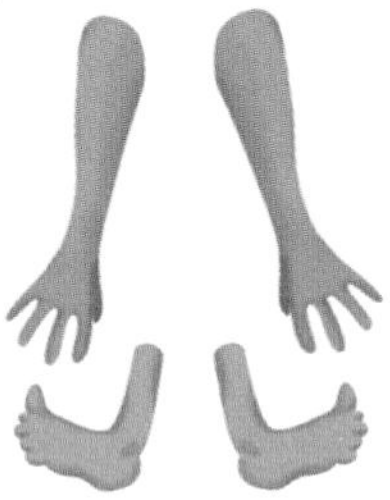

أَعْضَاءُ الْجِسْم
ʾaʿḍāʾul jism

line

khaṭṭ خَطّ

lion

ʾasad أَسَد

lip

shafah شَفَة

lipstick

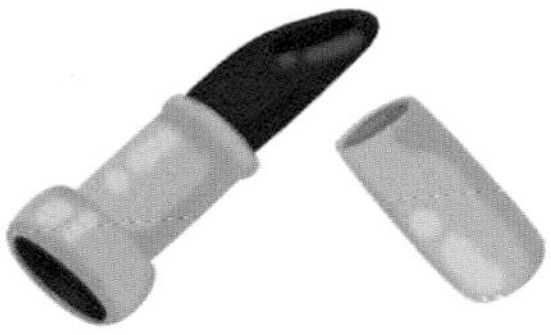

أَحْمَرُ الشِّفَاه
ʾaḥmarush shifāh

liquid

sāʾil سَائِل

list

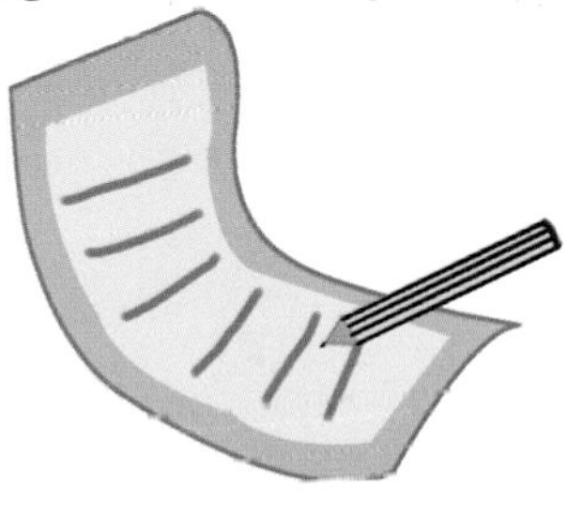

qāʾimah قَائِمَة

litre
US English **liter**

litr لِتْر

living room

غُرْفَةُ الْمَعِيْشَة
ghurfatul maʿīshah

lizard

sāmmu ʾabraṣa سَامُّ أَبْرَص

load

ḥiml\thiql حِمْل/ثِقْل

a b c d e f g h i j k l m n o p q r s t u v w x y z

loaf

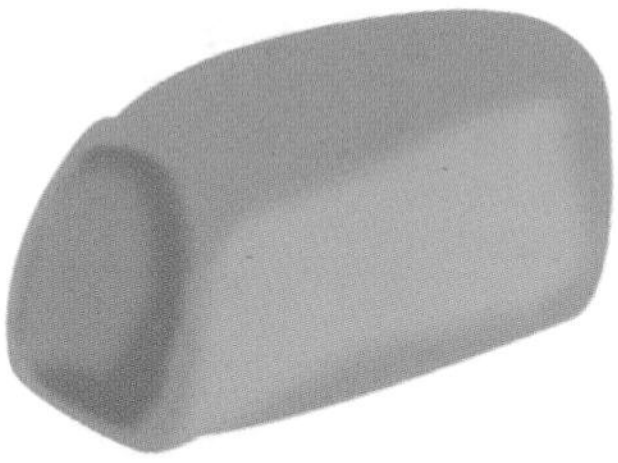

raghīf رَغِيْف

lobster

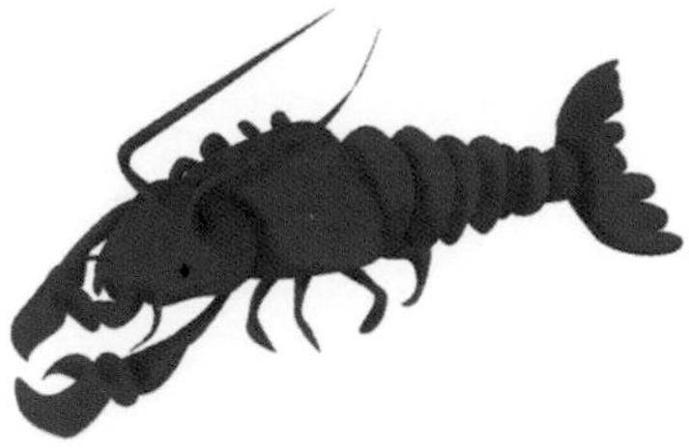

كَرْكَنْد/جَرَادُ الْبَحْر
karkand\jarādul baḥr

lock

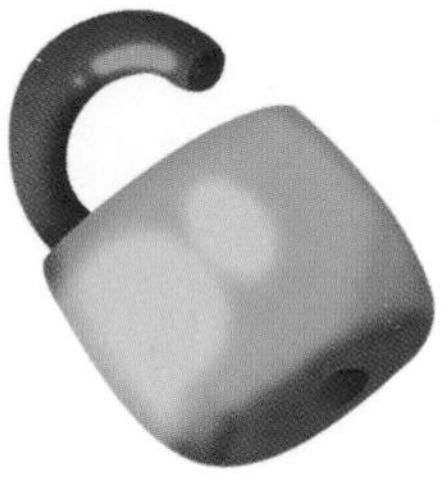

qufl قُفْل

loft

ʿulliyyah عُلِّيَّة

log

قِطْعَةُ خَشَب
qiṭʿatu khashab

loop

ʿurwah عُرْوَة

lorry

US English **truck**

shāḥinah شَاحِنَة

lotus

lūtus لُوْتُس

louse

qamlah قَمْلَة

luggage

ʾamtiʿah أَمتِعَة

lunch

ghadāʾ غَدَاء

lung

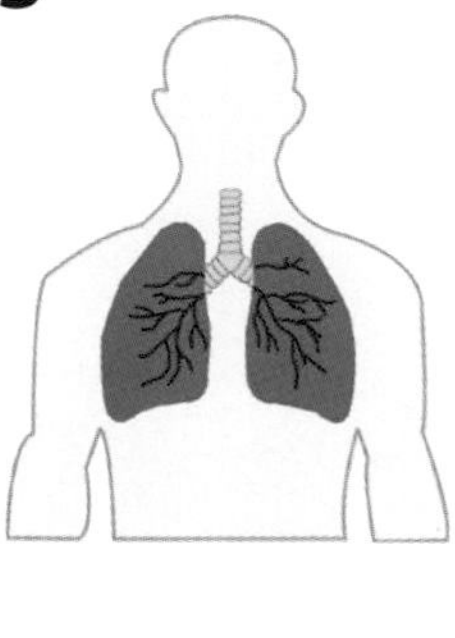

riʾah رِئَة

Mm

machine

آلَة/جِهَاز/مَاكِيْنَة
’ālah\jihāz\mākīnah

magazine

majallah مَجَلَّة

magician

sāḥir سَاحِر

magnet

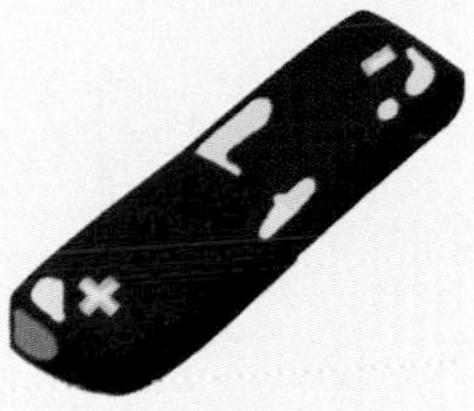

maghnaṭīs مَغْنَطِيْس

magpie

ʿaqʿaq عَقْعَق

mail

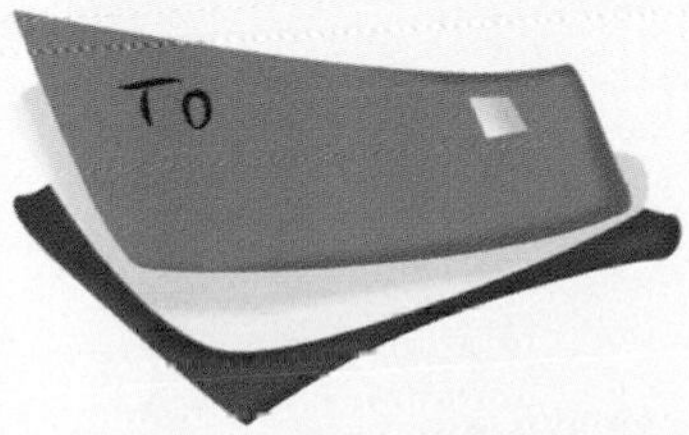

barīd بَرِيْد

mammal

حَيَوَان ثَدْيِيّ
ḥayawān thadyiyy

man

rajul رَجُل

mandolin

mandūlīn مَنْدُوْلِيْن

mango

مَنْجَة/أَنْبَج
manjah\’anbaj

map

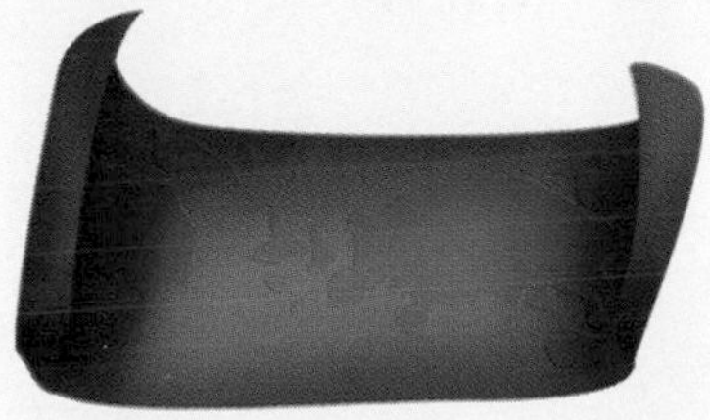

kharīṭah خَرِيْطَة

maple

qaiqab قَيْقَب

marble

كُرَة زُجَاجِيَّة
kurah zujājīyyah

market

sūq سُوْق

mask

قِنَاع/كِمَامَة
qināʿ\kimāmah

mast

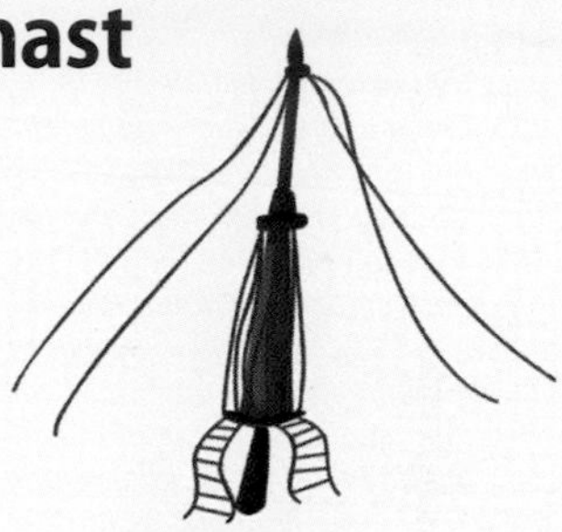

سَارِيَة/الصَّارِي
sāriyah\aṣṣārī

mat

mimsahah مِمْسَحَة

matchbox

عُلْبَةُ كِبْرِيْت
ʿulbatu kibrīt

mattress

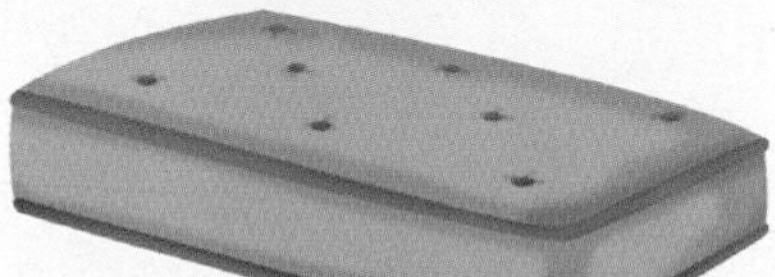

حَشِيَّة/فِرَاش
ḥashiyyah\firāsh

meal

wajbah وَجْبَة

meat

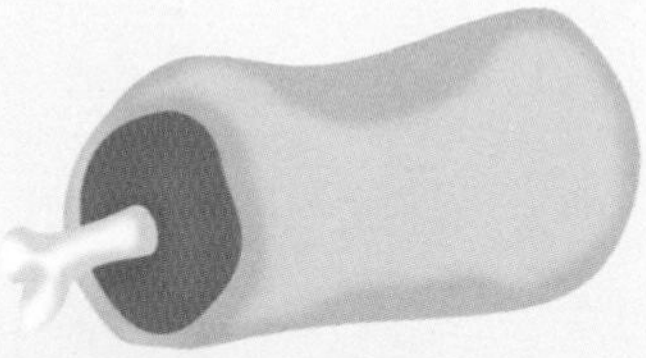

laḥm لَحْم

mechanic

mīkānīkī مِيْكَانِيْكِيّ

medicine

dawāʾ دَوَاء

melon

biṭṭīkh بِطِّيْخ

merchant

tājir تَاجِر

mermaid

حُوْرِيَّةُ الْبَحْر
ḥūriyyatul baḥr

metal

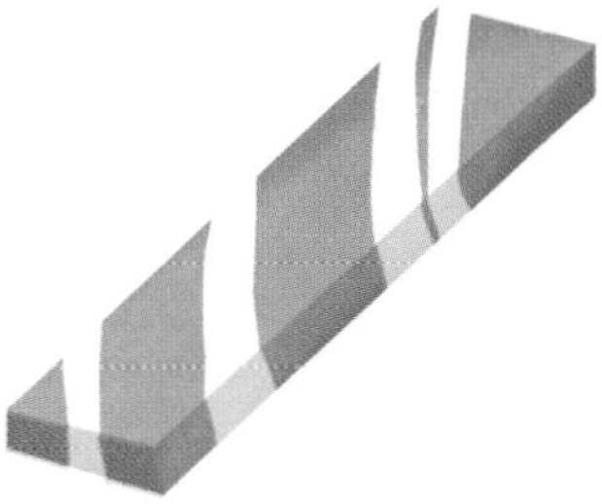

maʿdin مَعْدِن

metre

US English **meter**

mitr مِتْر

microphone

mīkrūfūn مِيْكْرُوْفُوْن

microwave

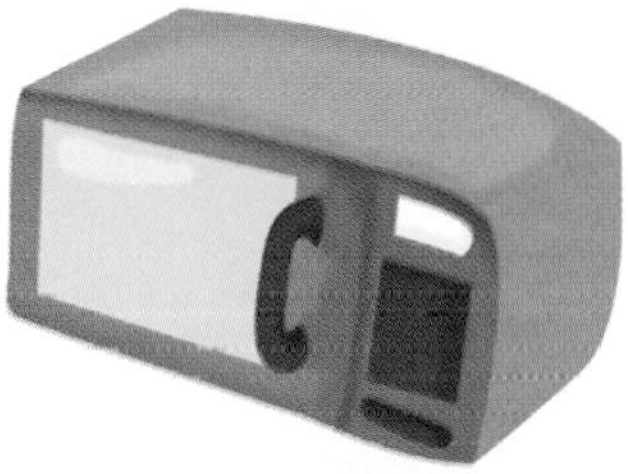

mīkrūwīf مِيْكْرُوْوِيْف

mile

mīl مِيْل

milk

laban\ḥalīb لَبَن/حَلِيْب

miner

ʿāmilu manjam عَامِلُ مَنْجَم

mineral

maʿdin مَعْدِن

mint

naʿnāʿ نَعْنَاع

minute

daqīqah دَقِيْقَة

mirror

mir'āt مِرْآة

mobile phone

جَوَّال/ هَاتِف مَحْمُوْل
jawwāl\hātif maḥmūl

model

'āriḍatu 'azyā' عَارِضَةُ أَزْيَاء

mole

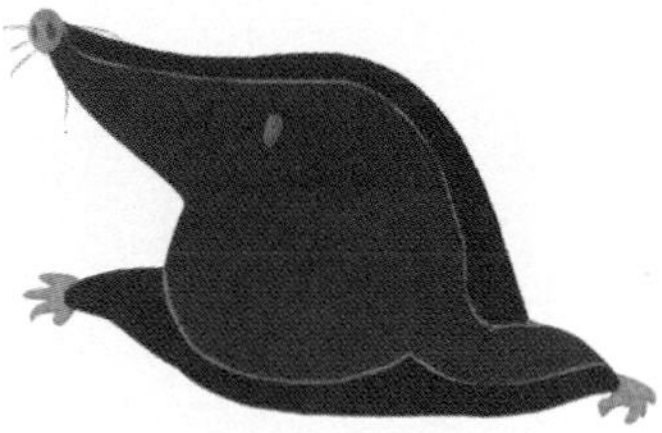

khuld خُلْد

money

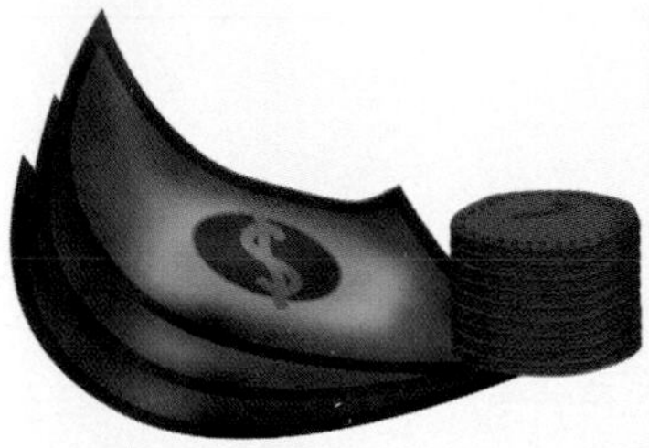

nuqūd\fulūs نُقُوْد/فُلُوْس

monk

rāhib رَاهِب

monkey

qird قِرْد

monster

maskh مَسْخ

month

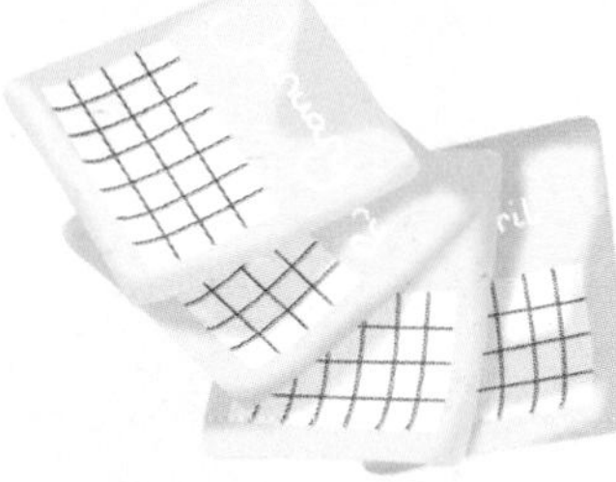

shahr شَهْر

monument

نُصُب تِذْكَارِيّ
nuṣub tidhkāriyy

moon

qamar قَمَر

mop

mimsaḥah مِمْسَحَة

morning

ṣabāḥ صَبَاح

mosquito

نَامُوْس/بَعُوْضَة
nāmūs\baʿūḍah

moth

عُثَّة/فَرَاشَة
ʿuththah\farāshah

mother

أُمّ/وَالِدَة
ʾumm\wālidah

motorcycle

دَرَّاجَة نَارِيَّة
darrājah nārīyyah

motorway

طَرِيْق سَرِيْع
ṭarīq sarīʿ

mountain

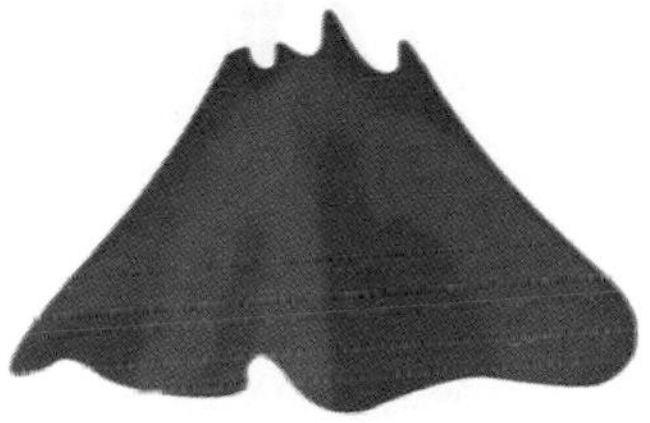

jabal جَبَل

mouse

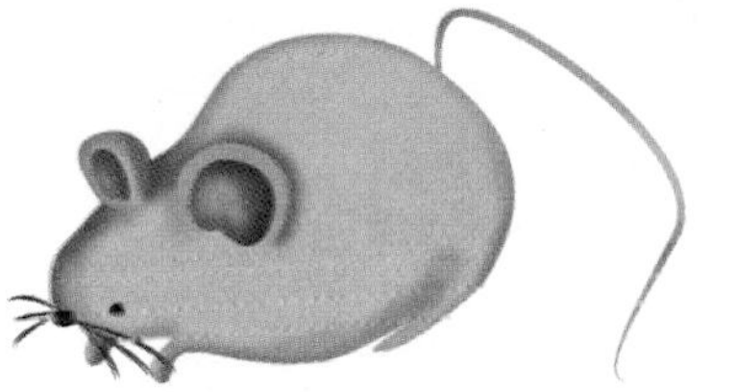

faʾrah فَأْرَة

mousetrap

مِصْيَدَةُ فِيْرَان
miṣyadatu fīrān

moustache

شَنَب/شَارِب
shanab\shārib

mouth

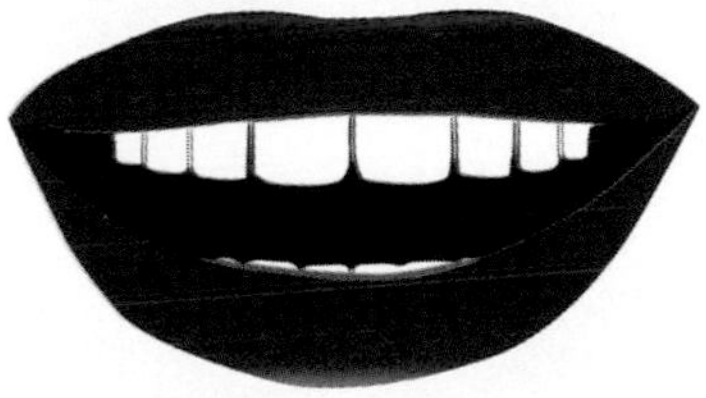

fam فَم

mud

waḥl وَحْل

muffin

mūfīn مُوْفِيْن

mug

kūz\kūb كُوْز/كُوْب

mule

baghl بَغْل

muscle

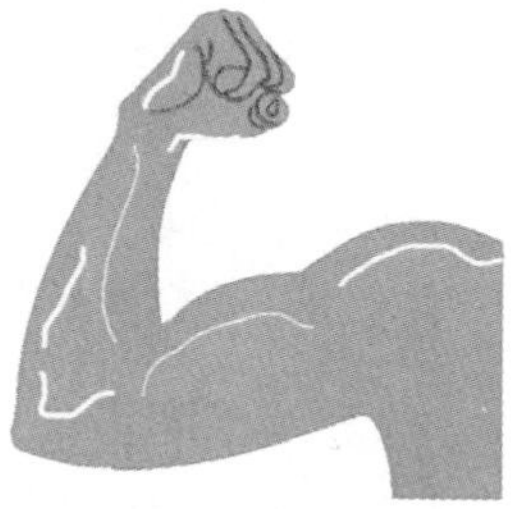

ʿaḍalah عَضَلَة

museum

matḥaf مَتْحَف

mushroom

fuṭr فُطْر

music

mūsīqa مُوْسِيْقَى

musician

mūsīqiyy مُوْسِيْقِيّ

Nn

nail

mismār مِسْمَار

napkin

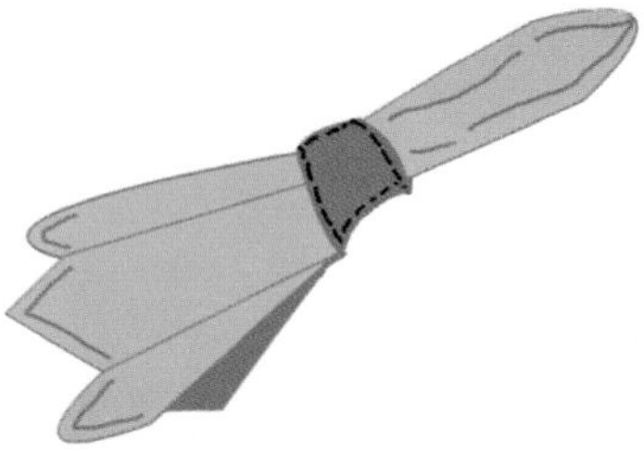

مِنْدِيْلُ الْمَائِدَة
mindīlul mā'idah

nappy
US English **diaper**

ḥifāẓuṭ ṭifl حِفَاظُ الطِّفْل

nature

ṭabīʿah طَبِيْعَة

neck

ʿunuq\raqabah عُنُق/رَقَبَة

necklace

ʿiqd\qilādah عِقْد/قِلَادَة

necktie

ribāṭul ʿunuq رِبَاطُ الْعُنُق

needle

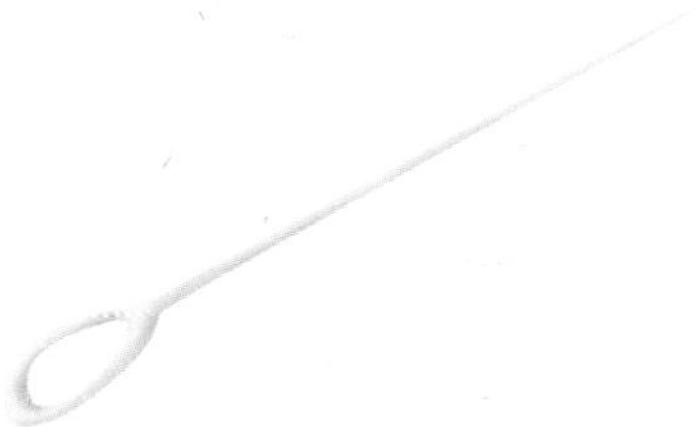

ʾibrah إِبْرَة

neighbour
US English **neighbor**

jār جَار

nest

ʿushsh\wakr عُشّ/وَكْر

net

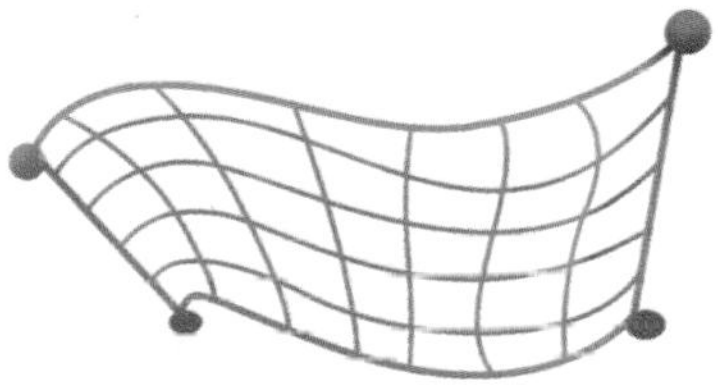

sharak شَرَك

newspaper

جَرِيْدَة/صَحِيْفَة
jarīdah\ṣaḥīfah

night

lail لَيْل

nine

tisʿah تِسْعَة

noodles

المَعْكَرُونَة/نُودِلْز

almaʿkrūnah\nūdilz

noon

ẓuhr ظُهْر

north

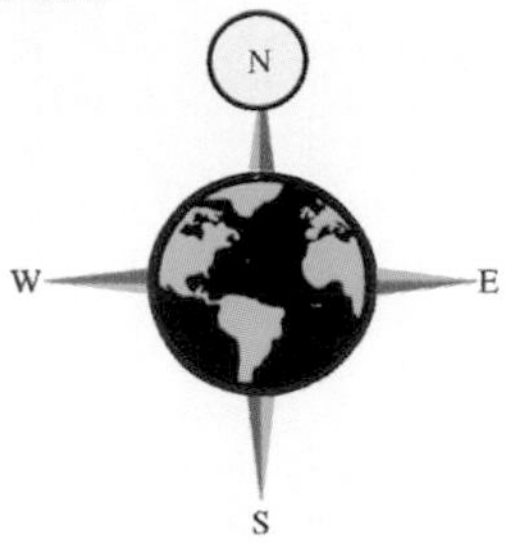

shimāl شِمَال

nose

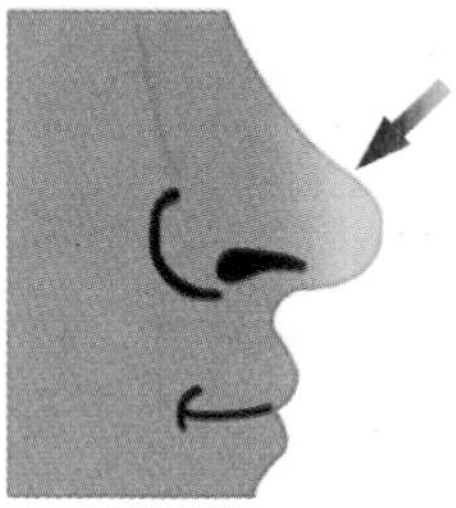

ʾanf أَنْف

note

mudhakkirah مُذَكِّرَة

notebook

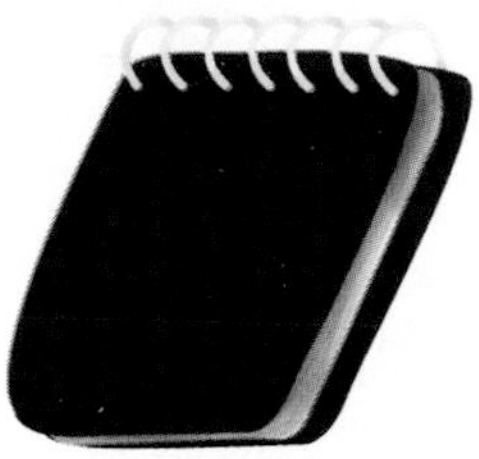

kurrāsah كُرَّاسَة

notice

ʾishʿār إِشْعَار

number

ʾarqām أَرْقَام

nun

rāhibah رَاهِبَة

nurse

mumarriḍah مُمَرِّضَة

nursery

ḥaḍānah حَضَانَة

nut

jauz جَوْز

Oo

oar

mijdhāf مِجْذَاف

observatory

marṣad مَرْصَدْ

ocean

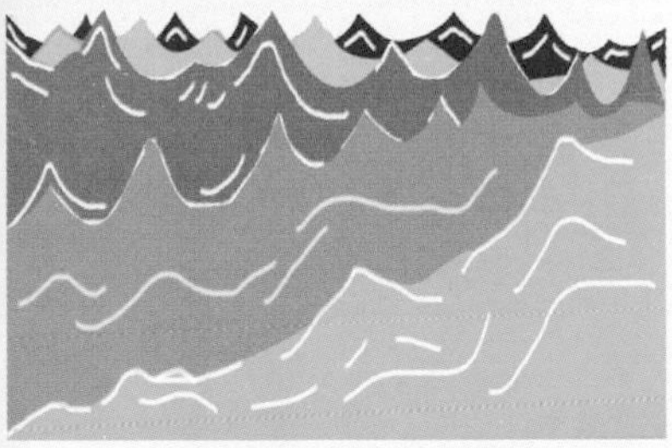

baḥr بَحْر

octopus

'ukhṭubūṭ أُخْطُبُوْط

office

maktab مَكْتَب

oil

zait زَيْت

olive

zaitūn زَيْتُوْن

omelette

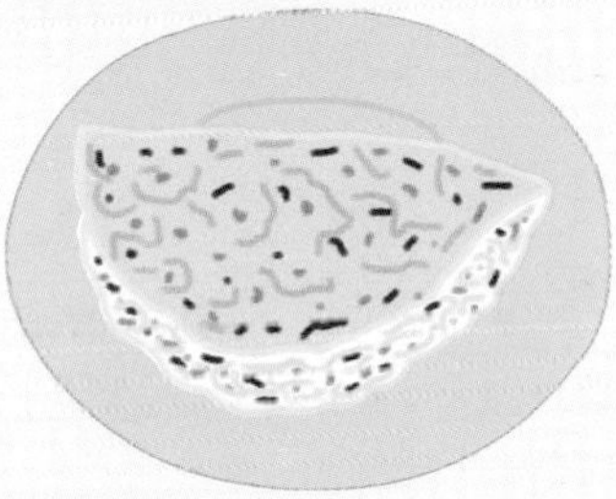

'ujjah عُجَّة

one

wāḥid وَاحِد

onion

baṣal بَصَل

orange

burtuqāl بُرْتُقَال

orbit

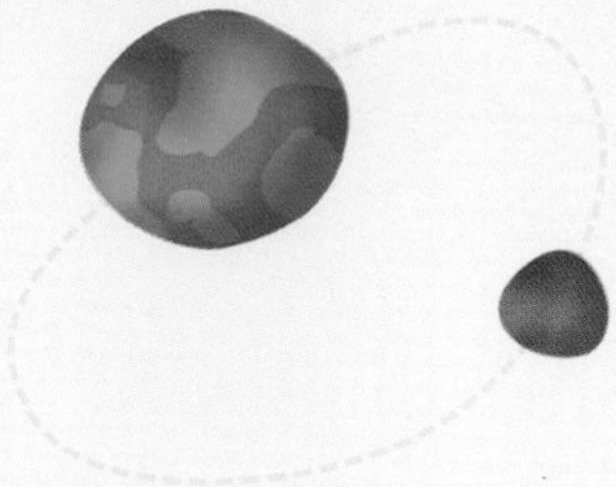

madār مَدَار

orchard

bustān بُسْتَان

orchestra

ʾūrkistarā أُورْكِسْتَرَا

ostrich

naʿāmah نَعَامَة

otter

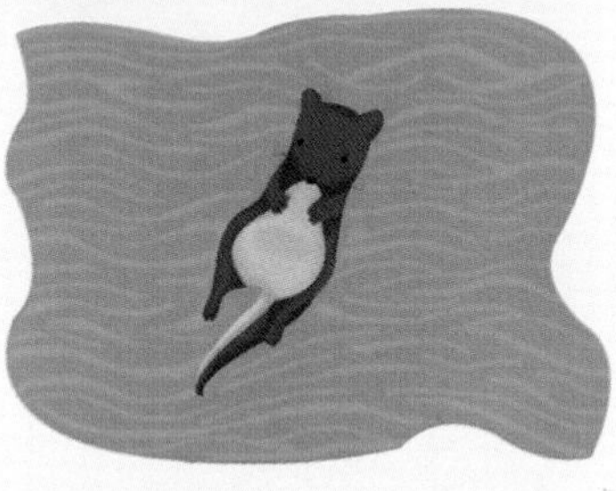

quḍāʿah قُضَاعَة

oval

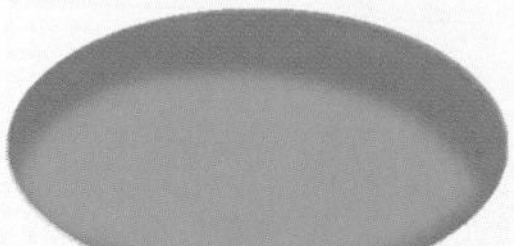

baiḍawiyy بَيْضَوِي

oven

furn فُرْن

owl

būmah بُومَة

ox

thaur ثَوْر

Pp

packet

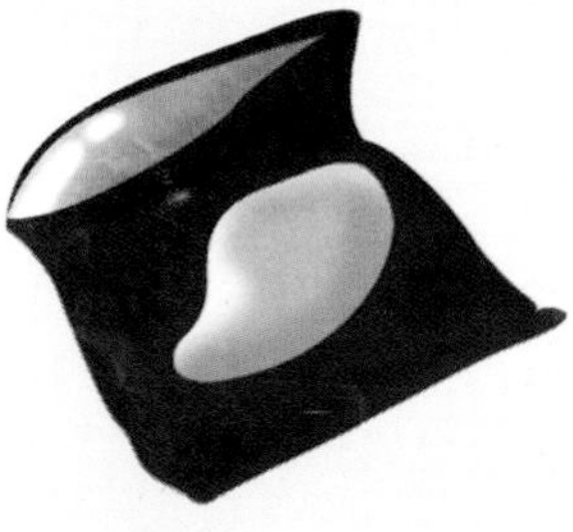

ruzmah رُزْمَة

page

ṣafḥah صَفْحَة

pain

ʾalam أَلَم

paint

dihān دِهَان

painting

rasm رَسْم

pair

zauj زَوْج

palace

qaṣr قَصْر

palm

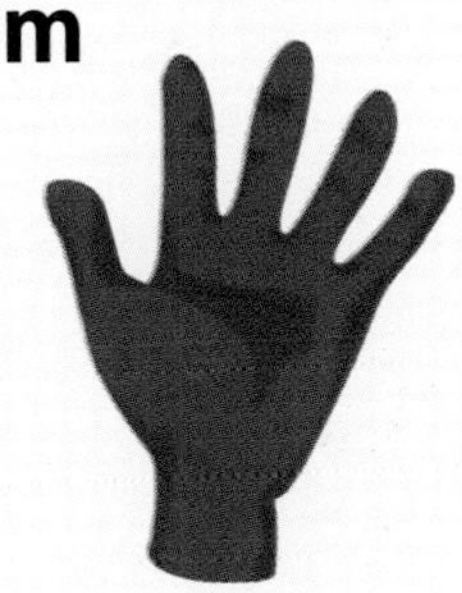

rāḥah رَاحَة

pan

miqlāt مِقْلَاة

pancake

فَطِيْرَة/زَلَابِيَة
faṭīrah\zalābiyah

panda

bandah بَنْدَة

papaya

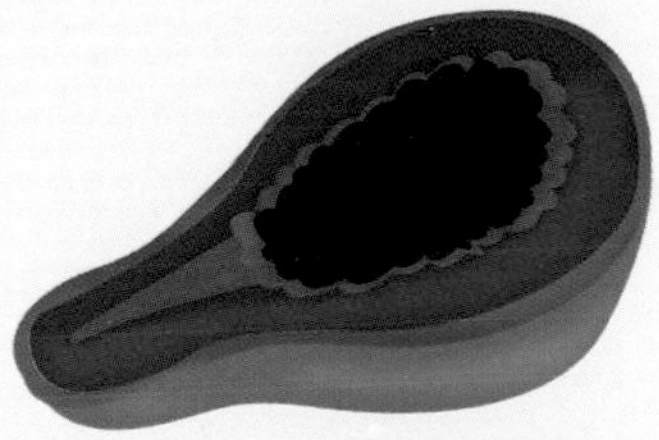

babaya بَبَايَا

paper

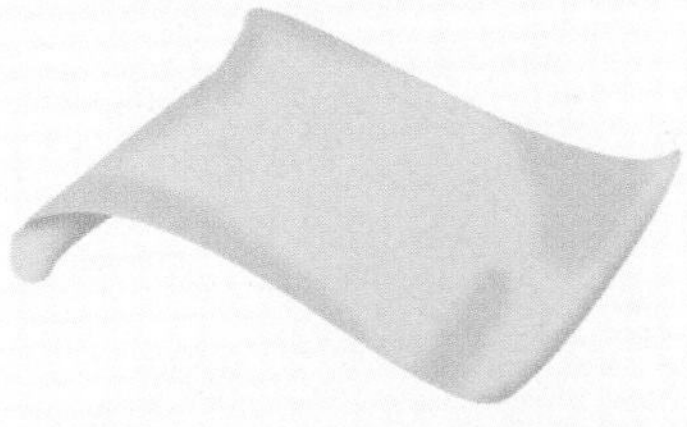

waraq وَرَق

parachute

مِظَلَّة/بَارَاشُوْت
miẓallah\bārāshūt

a b c d e f g h i j k l m n o p q r s t u v w x y z

parcel

ṭard طَرْد

park

مُتَنَزَّه/حَدِيْقَة
mutanazzah/ḥadīqah

parrot

babghā’ بَبْغَاء

passenger

rākib رَاكِب

pasta

bāstah بَاسْتَة

pastry

faṭīrah فَطِيْرَة

pavement

رَصِيْفُ الشَّارِع
raṣīfush shāriʿ

paw

بُرْثُن/مِخْلَب
burthun\mikhlab

pea

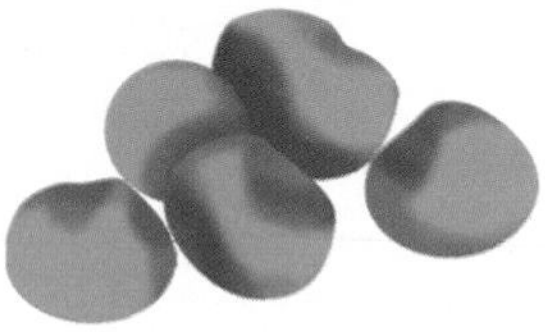

bāzillā بَازِلَّا

peach

khaukh خَوْخ

peacock

ṭā’ūs طَاوُوْس

peak

dhirwah\qimmah ذِرْوَة/قِمَّة

peanut

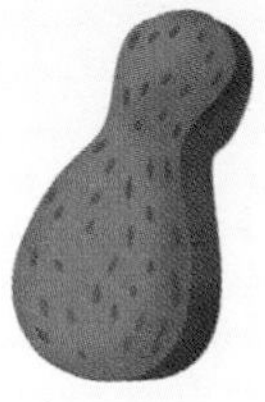

fūl sūdāni فُوْل سُوْدَانِي

pear

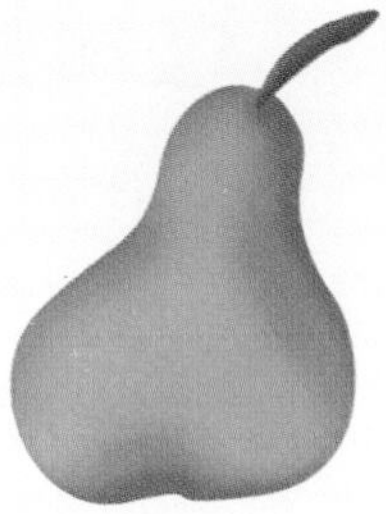

ʾijjāṣ إِجَّاص

pearl

luʾluʾ لُؤْلُؤ

pedal

dawwāsah دَوَّاسَة

pelican

bajaʿ بَجَع

pen

qalam قَلَم

pencil

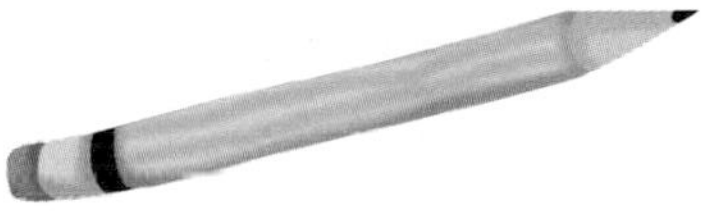

qalam raṣāṣ قَلَم رَصَاص

penguin

biṭrīq بِطْرِيْق

pepper

filfil فِلْفِل

perfume

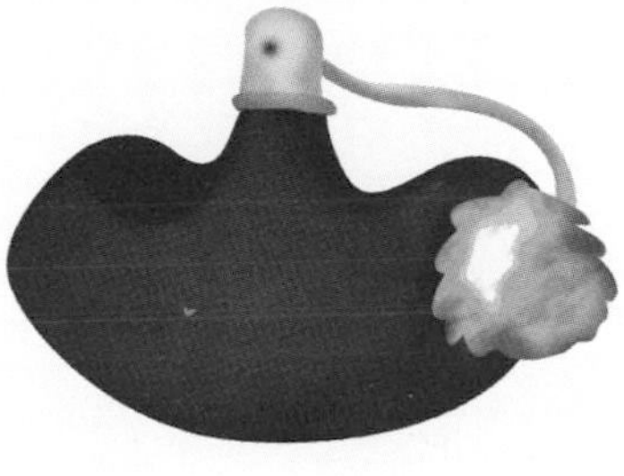

ʿiṭr عِطْر

pet

ḥayawān ʾalīf حَيَوَان أَلِيْف

pharmacy

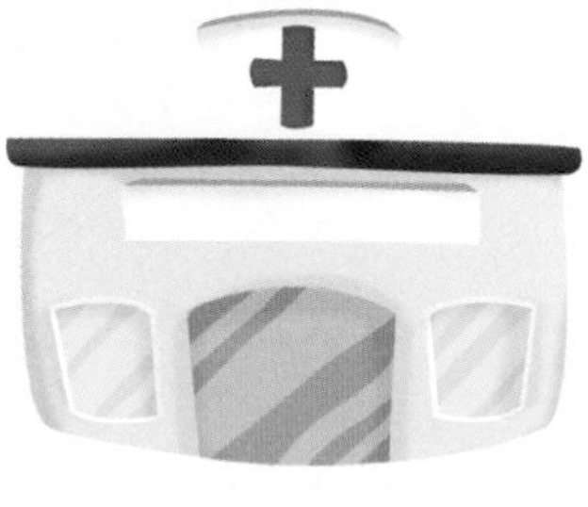

ṣaidaliyyah صَيْدَلِيَّة

photograph

ṣūrah صُوْرَة

piano

biyānū بِيَانُو

picture

rasm رَسْم

pie

faṭīrah فَطِيْرَة

pig

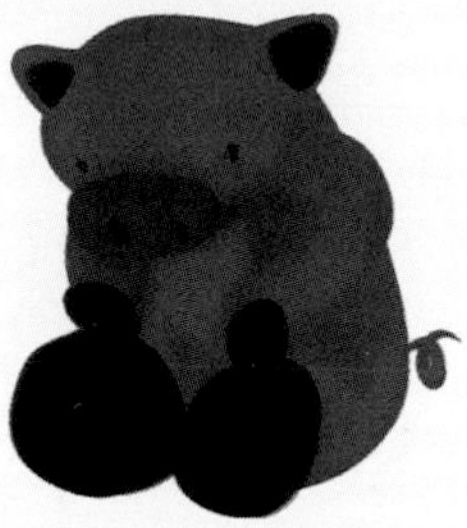

khinzīr خِنْزِيْر

pigeon

ḥamāmah حَمَامَة

pillar

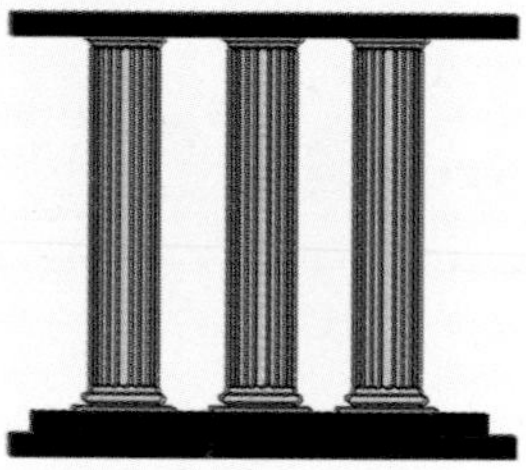

ʿamūd عَمُوْد

pillow

wisādah وِسَادَة

pilot

ṭayyār طَيَّار

pineapple

ʾanānās أَنَانَاس

pink

wardiyy وَرْدِيّ

pipe

ʾunbūb أُنْبُوْب

pizza

bītzā بِيْتْزَا

planet

kaukabah كَوْكَبَة

plant

gharsah غَرْسَة

plate
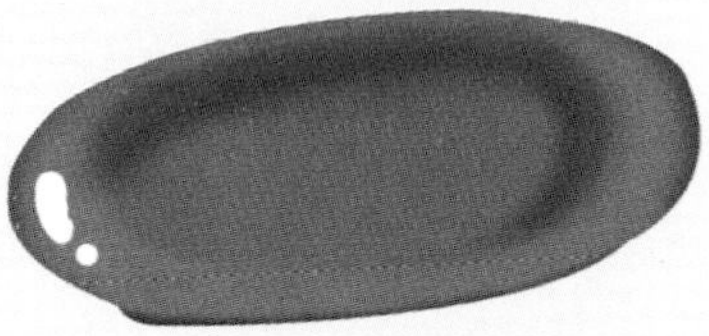
ṣaḥn\ṭabaq صَحْن/طَبَق

platform
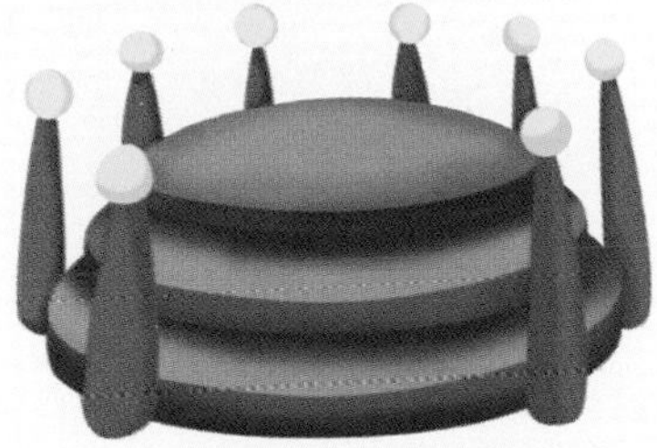
رَصِيْف/مِنَصَّة
raṣīf\minaṣṣah

platypus

bilānbūs بِلَانْبُوْس

player

lāʿib لَاعِب

plum

burqūq بُرْقُوْق

plumber

samkarī سَمْكَرِي

plywood

خَشَب رَقَائِقِي
khashab raqā'iqī

pocket

jaib جَيْب

poet

shāʿir شَاعِر

a b c d e f g h i j k l m n o **p** q r s t u v w x y z

polar bear

dubb quṭbī دُبّ قُطْبِي

police

shurṭah شُرْطَة

pollution

talawwuth تَلَوُّث

pomegranate

rummān رُمَّان

pond

birkah بِرْكَة

porcupine

naiṣ نَيْص

port

mīnā' مِيْنَاء

porter

ḥammāl\ʿattāl حَمَّال/عَتَّال

postcard

بِطَاقَةُ الْبَرِيْد
biṭāqatul barīd

postman

sāʿil barīd سَاعِي الْبَرِيْد

post office

maktabul barīd مَكْتَبُ الْبَرِيْد

pot

'aṣīṣ أَصِيْص

potato

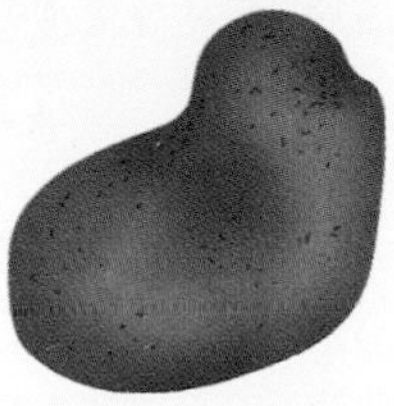

baṭāṭas بَطَاطَس

powder

بُوْدَرَة/مَسْحُوْق
būdarah\masḥūq

prawn

quraidis قُرَيْدِس

priest

kāhin كَاهِن

prince

ʾamīr أَمِيْر

prison

sijn سِجْن

pudding

būdīngh بُوْدِيْنغ

pump

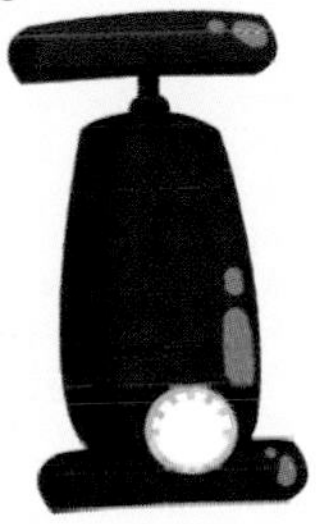

miḍakhkhah مِضَخَّة

pumpkin

yaqṭīn يَقْطِيْن

puppet

دُمْيَة مُتَحَرِّكَة
dumyah mutaharrikah

puppy

jarwul kalb جَرْوُ الْكَلْب

purse

kīsun nuqūd كِيْسُ النُّقُوْد

a b c d e f g h i j k l m n o p q r s t u v w x y z

Qq

quail

سُمَانَى/سَلْوَى
sumāna\salwa

quarry

maqlaʿ مَقْلَع

queen

malikah مَلِكَة

queue

ṣaff صَفّ

quiver

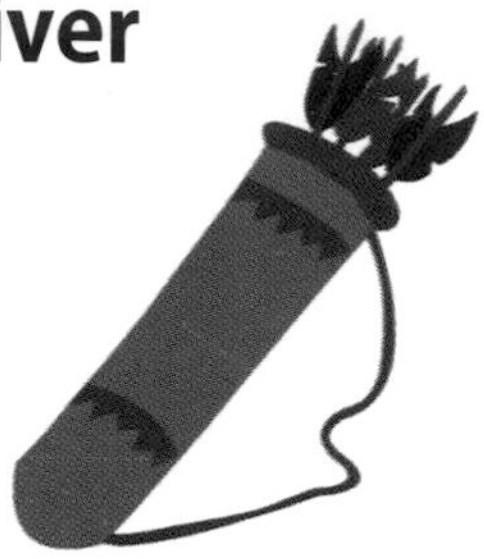

kinānah كِنَانَة

Rr

rabbit

ʾarnab أَرْنَب

rack

raff رَفّ

racket

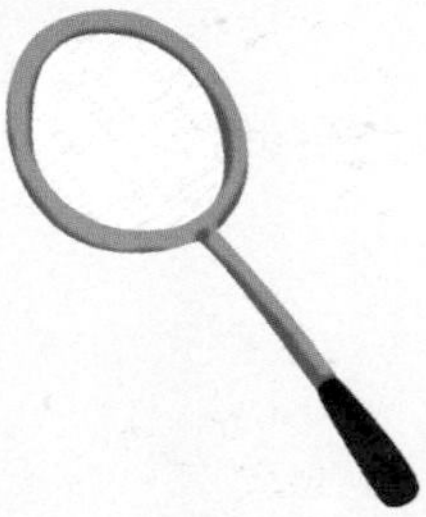

miḍrabut tinis مِضْرَبُ التِّنِس

radio

midhyāʿ مِذْيَاع

radish

fijl فِجْل

raft

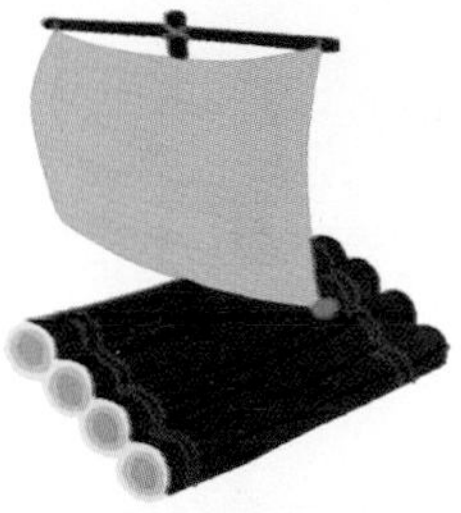

ramath\ṭauf رَمَث/طَوْف

rain

maṭar مَطَر

rainbow

qausu quzaḥ قَوْسُ قُزَح

raisin

zabīb زَبِيْب

ramp

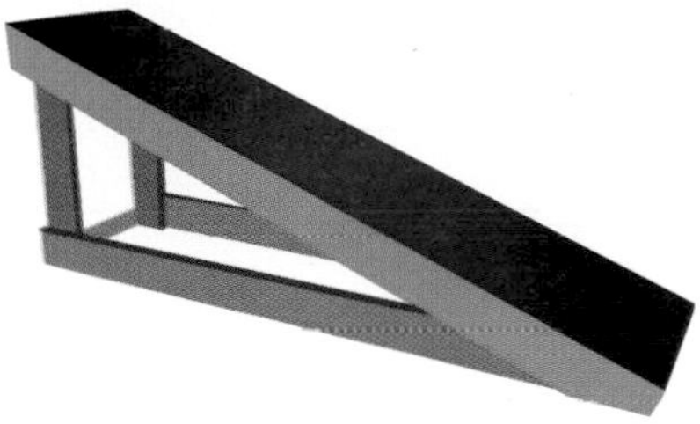

سَطْح مُنْحَدِر

saṭḥ munḥadir

raspberry

tutul ʿalīq تُوْت الْعَلِيْق

rat

faʾr فَأْر

razor

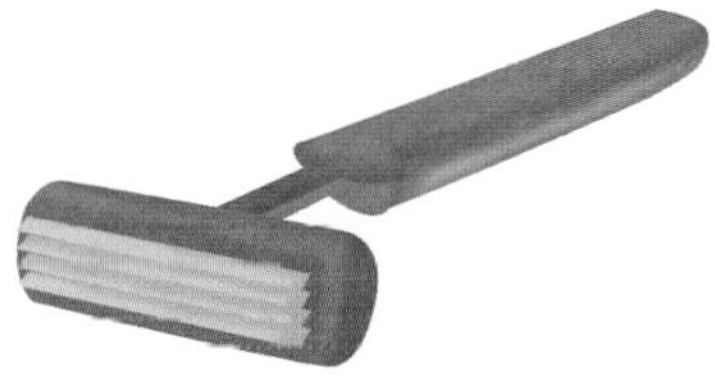

مُوْسى الْحِلَاقَة

mūsal ḥilāqah

receipt

waṣl وَصْل

rectangle

mustaṭīl مُسْتَطِيْل

red

ʾaḥmar أَحْمَر

restaurant

maṭʿam مَطْعَم

a b c d e f g h i j k l m n o p q r s t u v w x y z

rhinoceros

karkadan كَرْكَدَن

rib

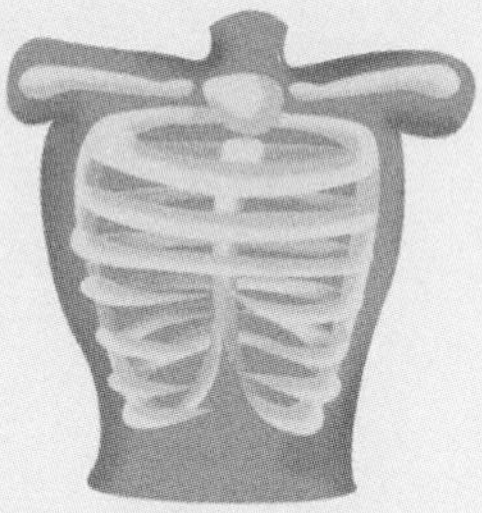

ḍilʿ ضِلْع

ribbon

sharīṭ شَرِيْط

rice

ʾaruzz أَرُزّ

ring

khātam خَاتَم

river

nahr نَهْر

road

ṭarīq طَرِيْق

robber

liṣṣ لِصّ

robe

ʿabāʾah عَبَاءة

robot

rūbūṭ رُوْبُوْط

rock

ṣakhr صَخْر

rocket

ṣārūkh صَارُوْخ

roller coaster

سَفِيْنَة دَوَّارة
safīnah dawwārah

room

غُرْفَة/حُجْرَة
ghurfah\ḥujrah

root

jidhr\judhūr جِذْر/جُذُوْر

rope

ḥabl حَبْل

rose

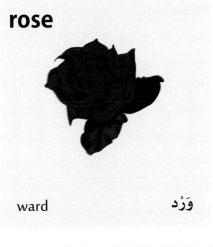

ward وَرْد

round

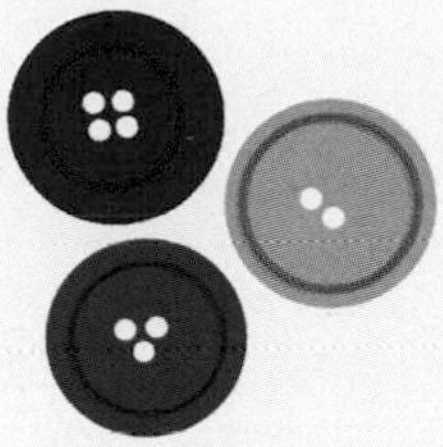

mustadīr مُسْتَدِيْر

rug

sajjādah سَجَّادَة

rugby

rūkbī رُوْكْبِي

ruler

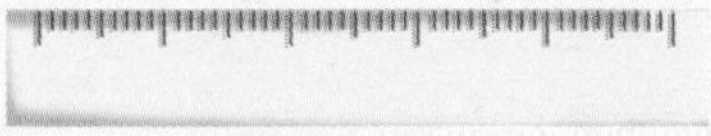

misṭarah مِسْطَرَة

Ss

sack

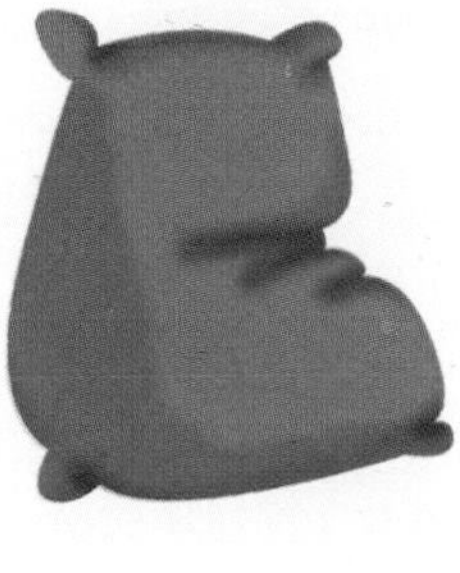

kīs كِيْس

sail

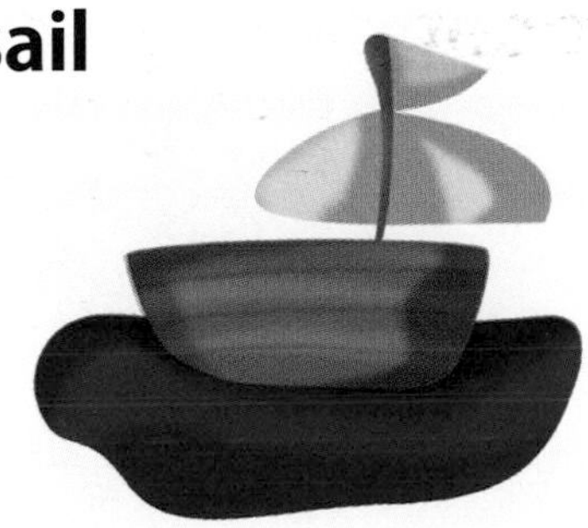

shirāʿ شِرَاع

a b c d e f g h i j k l m n o p q r s t u v w x y z

sailor

mallāḥ مَلَّاح

salad

salaṭah سَلَطَة

salt

milḥ مِلْح

sand

raml رَمْل

sandwich

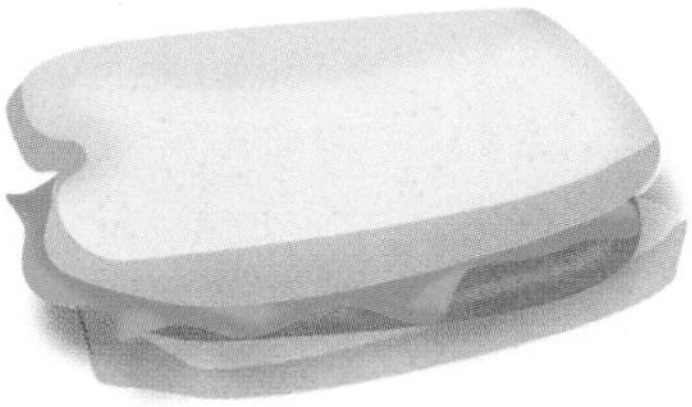

سَنْدْوِيْش/شَطِيْرَة
sandwīsh\shaṭīrah

satellite

قَمَر صِنَاعِيّ
qamar Ṣināʿiyy

saucer

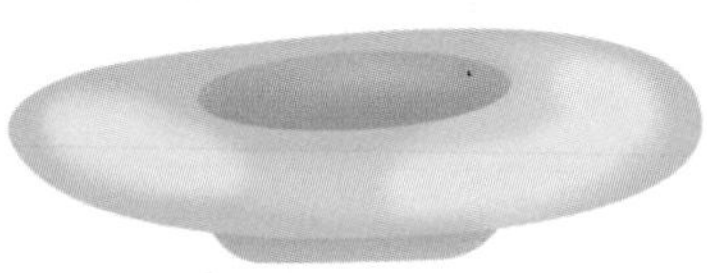

ṣuḥaifah صُحَيْفَة

sausage

naqāniq نَقَانِق

saw

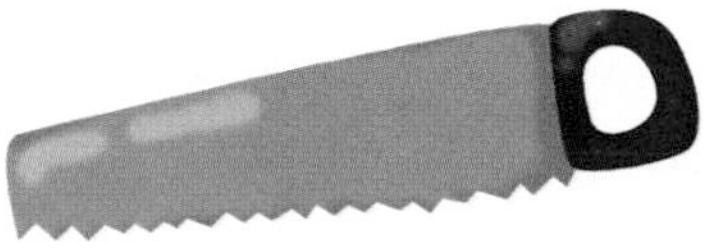

minshār مِنْشَار

scarf

لِفَاع/وِشَاح
lifāʿ\wishāḥ

school

madrasah مَدْرَسَة

scissors

مِقَصّ/مِقْرَاض
miqaṣṣ\miqrāḍ

scooter

iskūtar اِسْكُوْتَر

scorpion

ʿaqrab عَقْرَب

screw

laulab\burghī لَوْلَب/بُرْغِي

sea

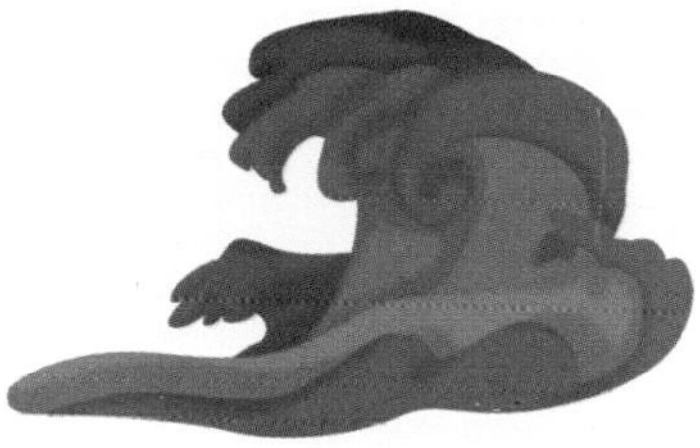

baḥr بَحْر

seal

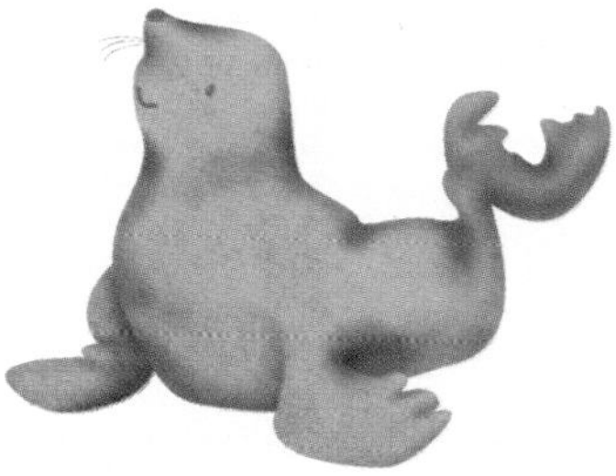

فُقْمَة/عِجْلُ الْبَحْر

fuqmah\ʿijlul baḥr

seat

maqʿad مَقْعَد

see-saw

nawwāsah نَوَّاسَة

seven

sabʿah سَبْعَة

shadow

ẓill ظِلّ

shampoo

shāmbū شَامْبُو

shark

qirsh قِرْش

sheep

kharūf\naʿjah خَرُوْف/نَعْجَة

shelf

raff رَفّ

shell

sadafah صَدَفَة

shelter

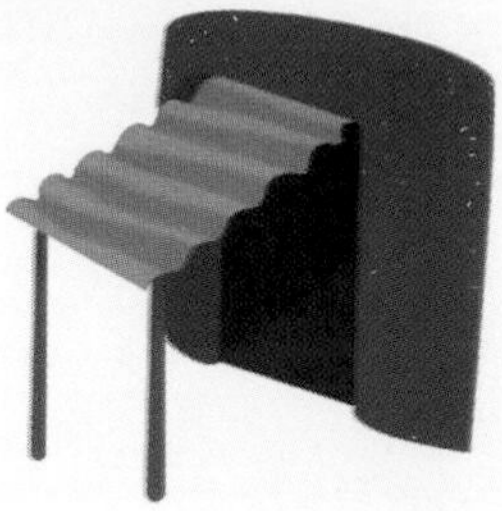

wiqāʾ وِقَاء

ship

safīnah سَفِيْنَة

shirt

qamīṣ قَمِيْص

shoe

hidhāʾ حِذَاء

shorts

شُوْرْت/سَلْوَارقَصِيْر
shūrt\salwār qaṣīr

shoulder

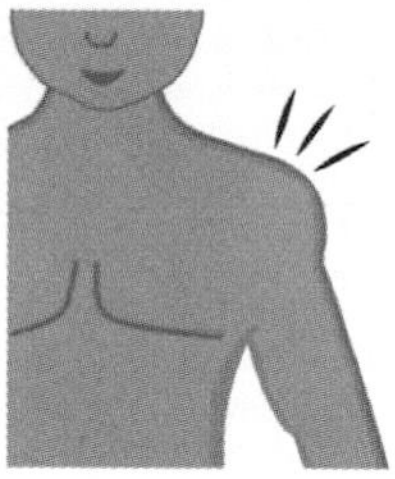

كَتِف/مَنْكِب
katif\mankib

shower

دُش/رَشَّاشَة
dush\rashshāshah

shutter

miṣrāʿ مِصْرَاع

shuttlecock

shaṭkūk شَطْكُوْك

signal

ʾishāratu murūr إِشَارَةُ مُرُوْر

silver

fiḍḍah\lujain فِضَّة/لُجَيْن

sink

maghsalah مَغْسَلَة

sister

’ukht أُخْت

six

sittah سِتَّة

skate

mizlaq\mizlaj مِزْلَق/مِزْلَج

skeleton

haikal ‘azmiyy هَيْكَل عَظْمِيّ

ski

tazaḥluq تَزَحْلُق

skin

jild جِلْد

skirt

tanūrah تَنُوْرَة

skull

jumjumah جُمْجُمَة

sky

samā’ سَمَاء

skyscraper

نَاطِحُ السَّحَاب
nāṭiḥus saḥāb

slide

mazlaq مَزْلَق

slipper

shibshib شِبْشِب

smoke

dukhān دُخَان

snail

حَلَزُوْن/بَزَّاقَة
ḥalazūn\bazzāqah

snake

ḥayyah حَيَّة

snow

thalj ثَلْج

soap

ṣābūn صَابُوْن

sock
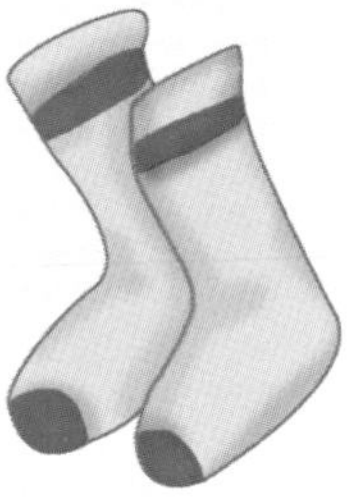

jaurab جَوْرَب

sofa

ʾarīkah أَرِيْكَة

soil
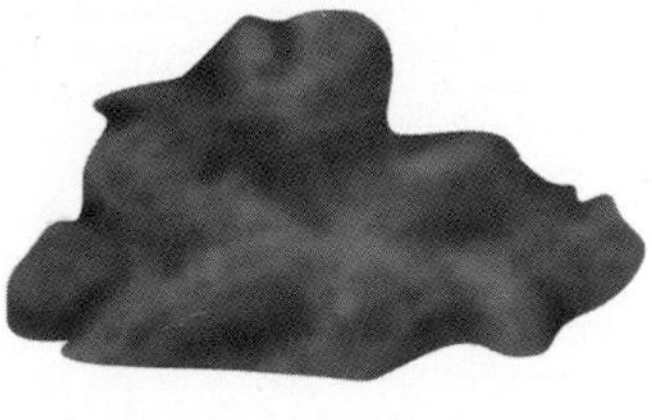

turāb تُرَاب

soldier

jundiyy جُنْدِيّ

soup

ḥasāʾ حَسَاء

space

faḍā' فَضَاء

spaghetti

sibāghītī سِبَاغِيْتِي

sphere

kurawiyy كُرَوِيّ

spider

ʿankabūt عَنْكَبُوْت

spinach

isfānākh إِسْفَانَاخ

sponge

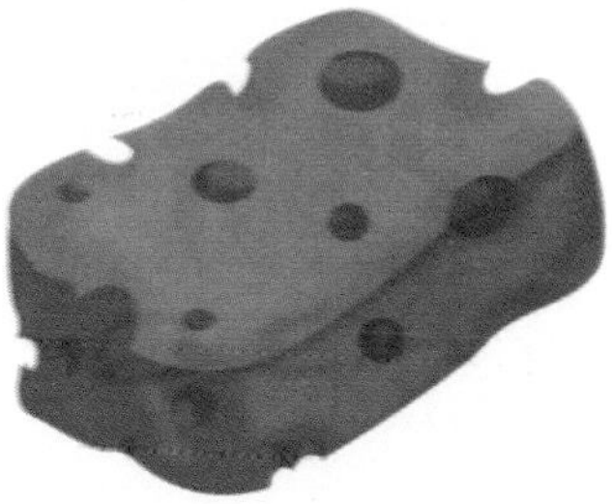

'isfanj إِسْفَنْج

spoon

milʿaqah مِلْعَقَة

spray

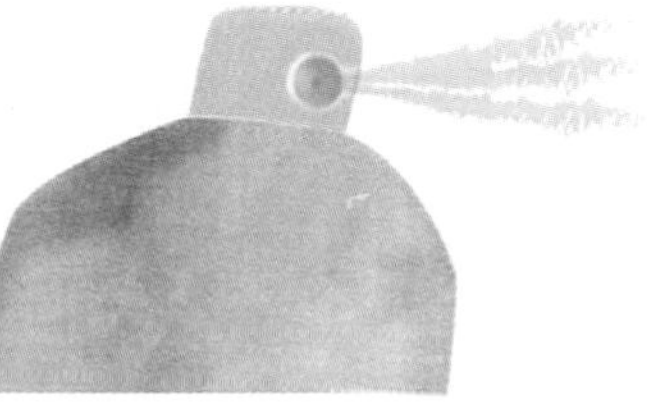

mirashshah مِرَشَّة

spring

rabīʿ رَبِيْع

square

murabbaʿ مُرَبَّع

squirrel

sinjāb سِنْجَاب

stadium

'istād\mal'ab إِسْتَاد/مَلْعَب

stairs

salālim سَلَالِم

stamp

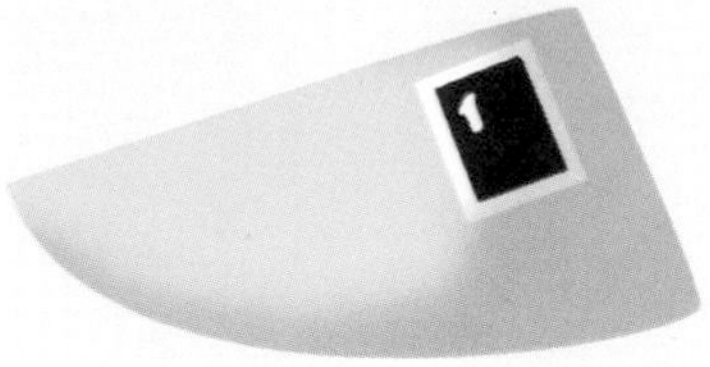

ṭābaʿu barīd طَابَعُ بَرِيْد

star

najm نَجْم

station

maḥattah مَحَطَّة

statue

timthāl تِمْثَال

stethoscope

sammāʿah سَمَّاعَة

stomach

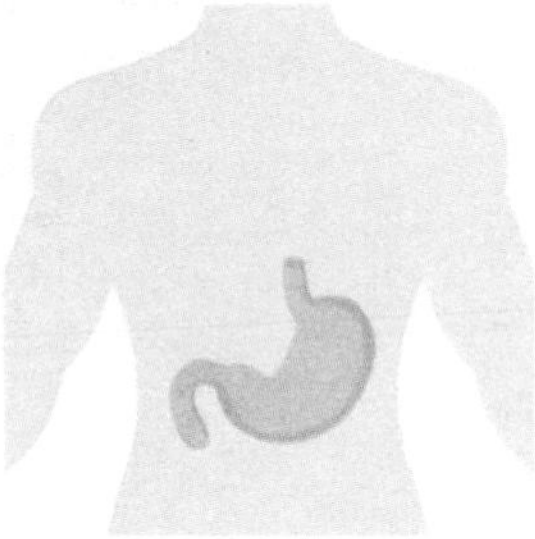

maʿidah مَعِدَة

stone

ḥajar حَجَر

storm

ʿāṣifah عَاصِفَة

straw

ashshārūqah الشَّارُوْقَة

strawberry

فَرَاوْلَة/تُوْت أَرْضِيّ
farāwlah\tūt ʾarḍiyy

street

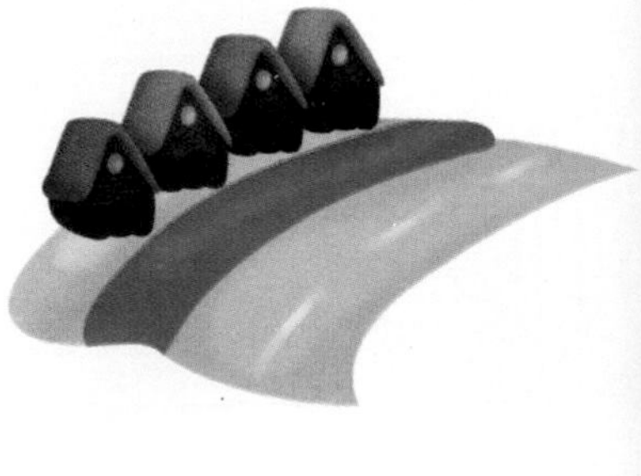

shāriʿ شَارِع

student

tilmīdh/ṭālib تِلْمِيْذ/طَالِب

submarine

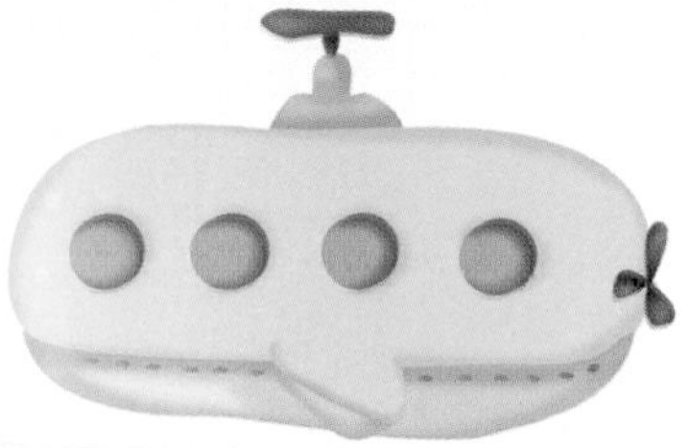

ghawwāṣah غَوَّاصة

subway

الْقِطَار الكَهْرَبَائِيّ النَّفَقِيّ
alqiṭārul kahrabā'iyyun nafaqiyy

sugar

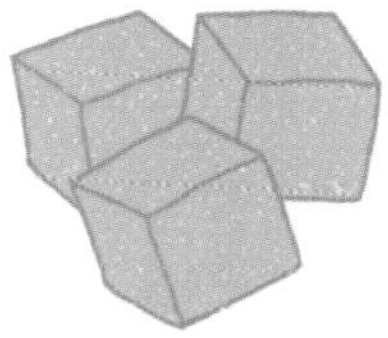

sukkar سُكَّر

sugarcane

قَصَبُ السُّكَّر
qaṣabus sukkar

summer

ṣaif صَيْف

sun

shams شَمْس

supermarket

سُوْق مَرْكَزِيَّة
sūq markaziyyah

swan

تَمّ/الإِوَزُّ الْعِرَاقِي
tamm\al'iwazzul ʿirāqī

sweet

ḥulwiyyāt حُلْوِيَّات

swimming pool

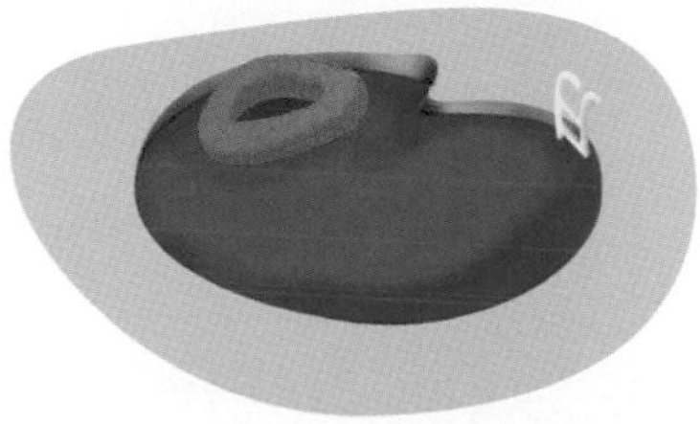

حَوْض السِّبَاحَة
ḥauḍus sibāḥah

swimsuit

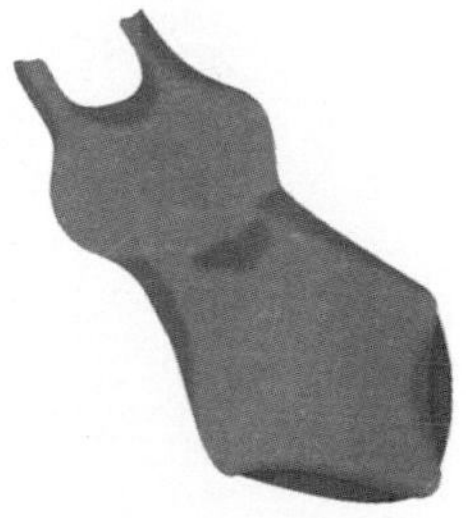

مَايُو/ثَوْبُ السِّبَاحَة
māyū\thaubus sibāḥah

swing

ʾurjūḥah أُرْجُوحَة

switch

zurr\miftāḥ زُرّ/مِفْتَاح

syrup

sharāb شَرَاب

Tt

table

طَاوِلَة/مِنْضَدَة
ṭāwilah\minḍadah

tall

ṭawīl طَوِيل

tank

dabbābah دَبَّابَة

taxi

tāksī تَاكْسِي

tea

shāy شَاي

teacher

مُدَرِّس/مُعَلِّم
mudarris\muʿallim

teeth

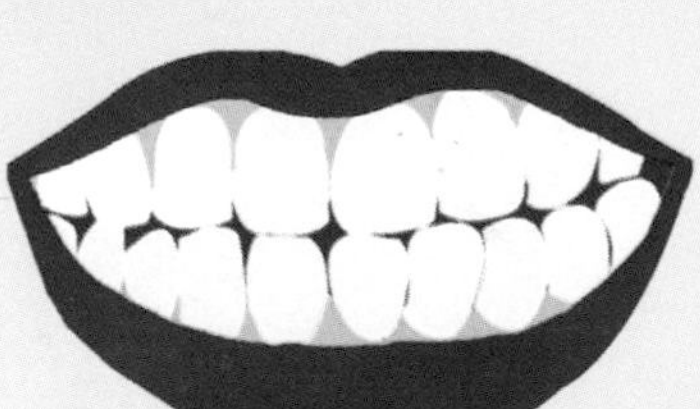

ʾasnān أَسْنَان

telephone

tilīfūn\hātif تِلِيفُون/هَاتِف

television

tilfizyūn تِلْفِزْيُوْن

ten

ʿasharah عَشَرَة

tennis

tinis تِنِس

tent

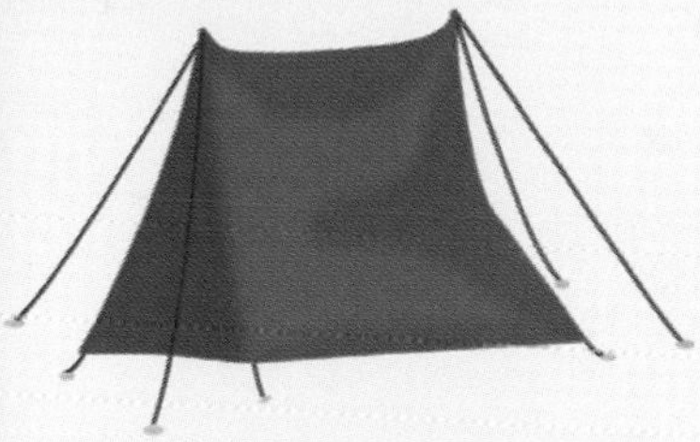

khaimah خَيْمَة

thief

sāriq\liṣṣ سَارِق/لِصّ

thread

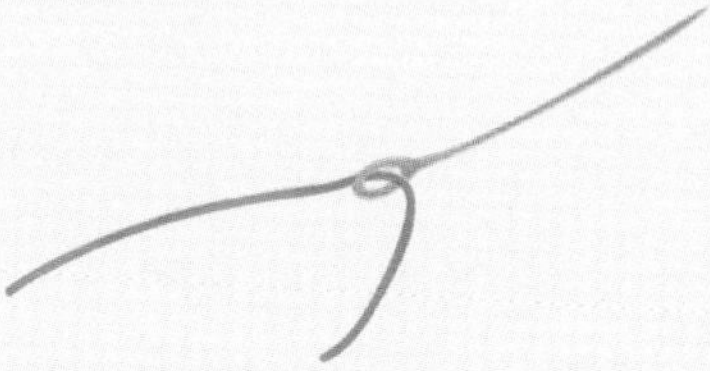

khaiṭ خَيْط

three

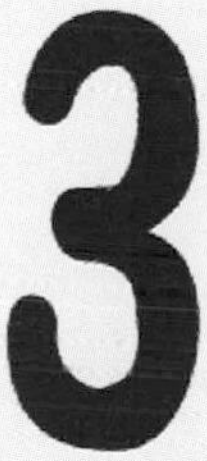

thalāthah ثَلَاثَة

throat

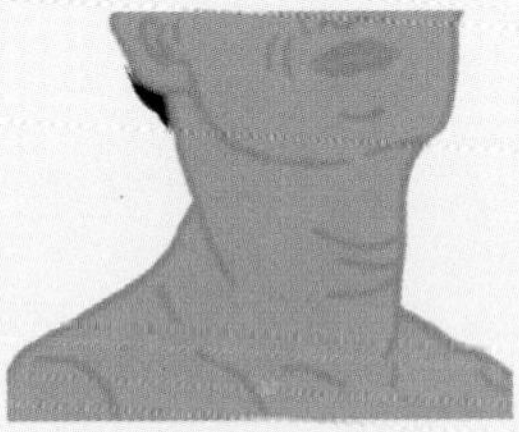

ḥalaq حَلَق

thumb

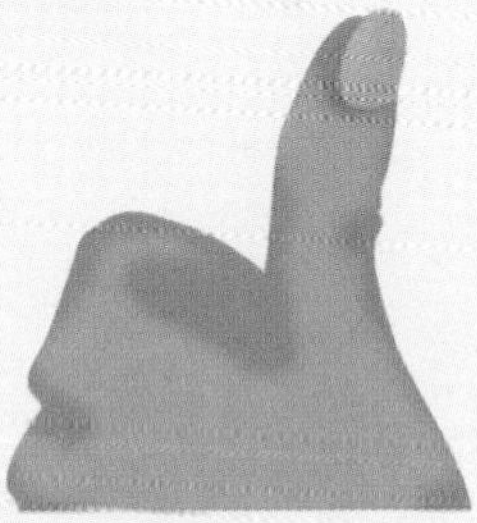

ʾibhām إِبْهَام

ticket

tadhkirah تَذْكِرَة

tiger

namir نَمِر

toe

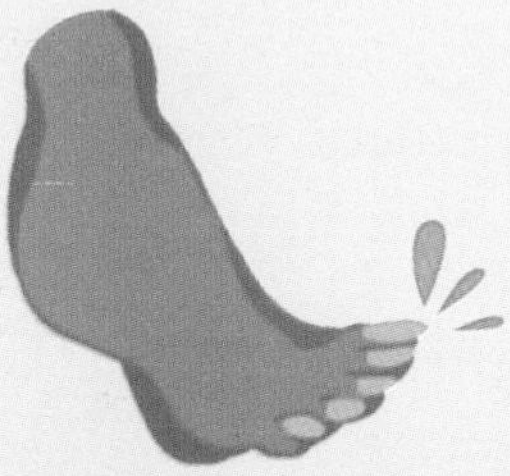

ʾisbaʿul qadam إِصْبَعُ الْقَدَم

a b c d e f g h i j k l m n o p q r s **t** u v w x y z

tofu

tūfū\ṣūyā تُوْفُو/صُوْيَا

tomato

ṭamāṭam طَمَاطَم

tongue

lisān لِسَان

tool

ʾadawāt أَدَوَات

toothbrush

فُرْشَةُ أَسْنَان
furshatu ʾasnān

toothpaste

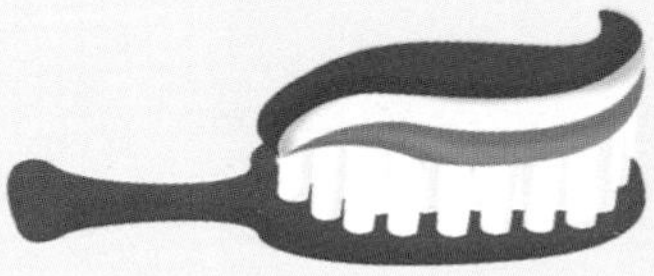

مَعْجُوْنُ أَسْنَان
maʿjūnu ʾasnān

tortoise

sulaḥfāt سُلَحْفَاة

towel

minshafah مِنْشَفَة

tower

burj بُرْج

toy

luʿbah لُعْبَة

tractor

جَرَّارَة/تِرَاكْتُوْر
jarrārah\tirāktūr

train

qiṭār قِطَار

tree

shajarah شَجَرَة

triangle

muthallath مُثَلَّث

tub

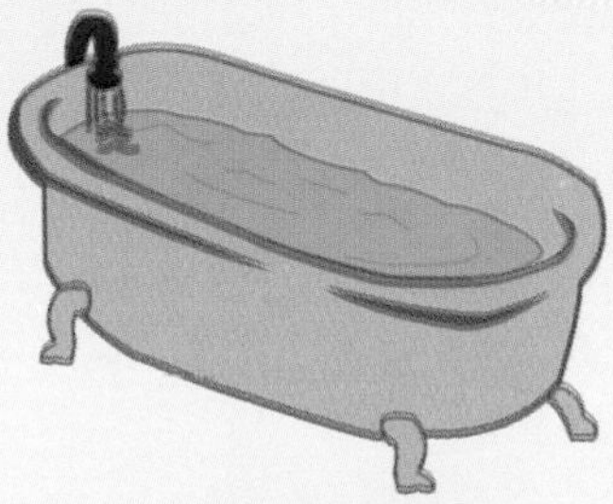

حَوْضُ اِسْتِحْمَام
ḥauḍu istiḥmām

tunnel

nafaq نَفَق

turnip

lift لِفْت

tyre
US English **tire**

'iṭāru sayyārah إِطَارُ سَيَّارَة

Uu

umbrella

شَمْسِيَّة/مِظَلَّة
shamsiyyah\miẓallah

uncle

ʿamm عَمّ

uniform

ziyy rasmiyy زِيّ رَسْمِي

university

jāmiʿah جَامِعَة

utensil

'āniyah آنِيَة

a
b
c
d
e
f
g
h
i
j
k
l
m
n
o
p
q
r
s
t
u
v
w
x
y
z

Vv

vacuum cleaner

مِكْنَسَة كَهْرَبَائِيَّة
miknasah kahrabā'iyyah

valley

alwādī الْوَادِي

van

sayyāratu naql سَيَّارَةُ نَقْل

vase

زَهْرِيَّة/مَزْهَرِيَّة
zahriyyah\mazhariyyah

vault

سَرْدَاب/قَبْو
sardāb\qabw

vegetable

khuḍar خُضَر

veil

ḥijāb حِجَاب

vet

baiṭariyy بَيْطَرِي

village

qaryah قَرْيَة

violet

banafsajiyy بَنَفْسَجِي

violin

kamān كَمَان

volcano

burkān برْكان

volleyball

kuratul yad كُرَةُ الْيَد

vulture

nasr نَسْر

Ww

waist
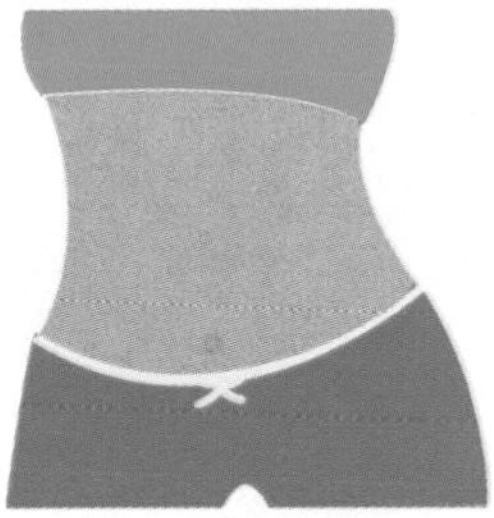

khaṣr خَصْر

waitress

nādilah نَادِلَة

wall

ḥā'iṭ\jidār حَائِط/جِدَار

wallet
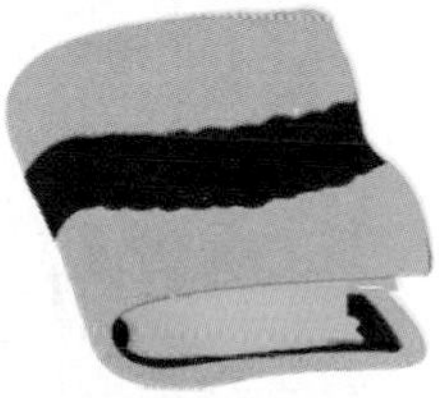

miḥfaẓatu jaib مِحْفَظَةُ جَيْب

walnut

jauz جَوْز

wand

عصًى سِحْرِيَّة
ʿasa siḥriyyah

wardrobe

خِزَانَةُ الثِّيَاب
khizānatuth thiyāb

warehouse
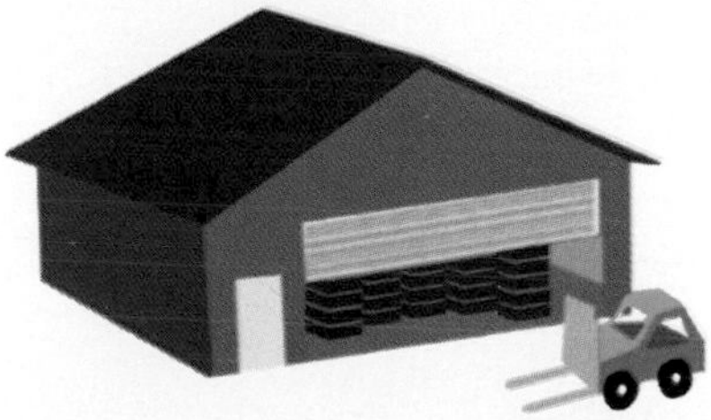

mustaudaʿ مُسْتَوْدَع

wasp

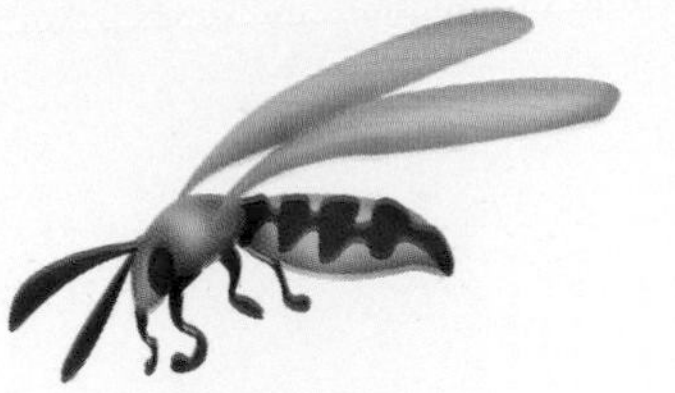

zunbūr زُنْبُور

watch

sāʿah سَاعَة

water

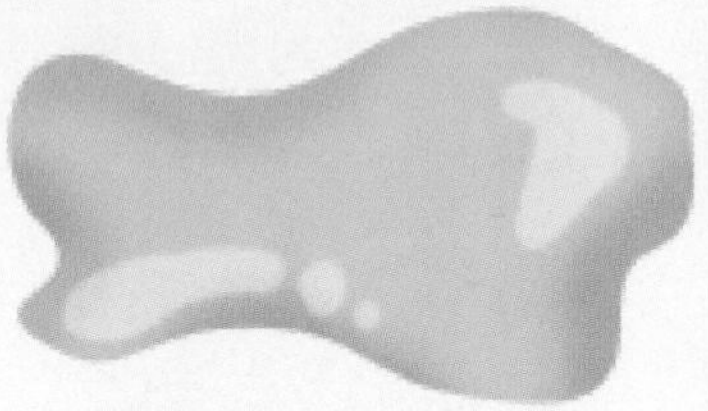

māʾ مَاء

watermelon

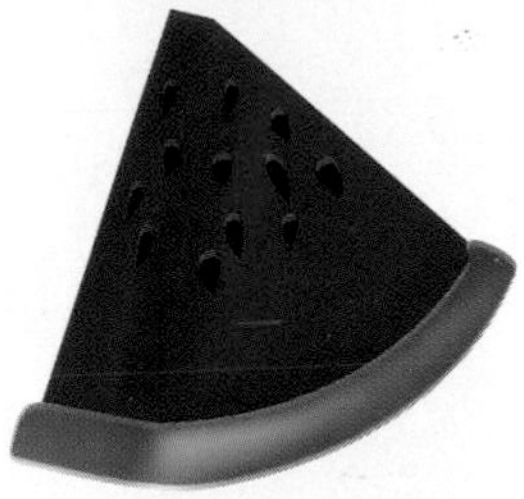

biṭṭīkh ʾaḥmar بِطِّيْخ أَحْمَر

web

نَسِيْجُ عَنْكَبُوْت
nasīju ʿankabūt

whale

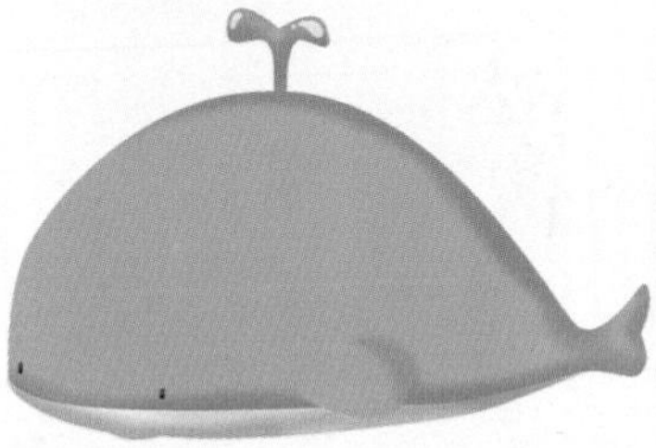

ḥūt حُوْت

wheat

qamḥ قَمْح

wheel

عَجَلَة/دُوْلَاب
ʿajalah\dūlāb

whistle

ṣaffārah صَفَّارَة

white

ʾabyaḍ أَبْيَض

wife

زَوْجَة/قَرِيْنَة
zaujah\qarīnah

window

شُبَّاك/نَافِذَة
shubbāk\nāfidhah

wing

janāḥ جَنَاح

winter

shitā’ شِتَاء

wizard

sāḥir سَاحِر

wolf

dhi’b ذِئْب

woman

imra’ah اِمْرَأَة

woodpecker

نَقَّار/قَرَّاع
naqqār\qarrāʿ

wool

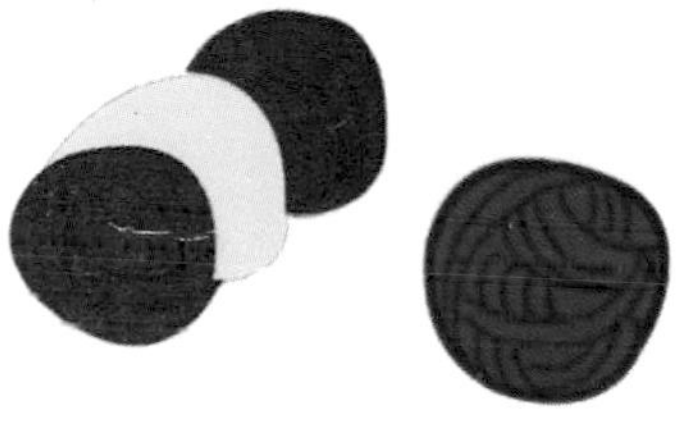

ṣūf صُوْف

workshop

وَرْشَة/مَعْمَل
warshah\maʿmal

wrist

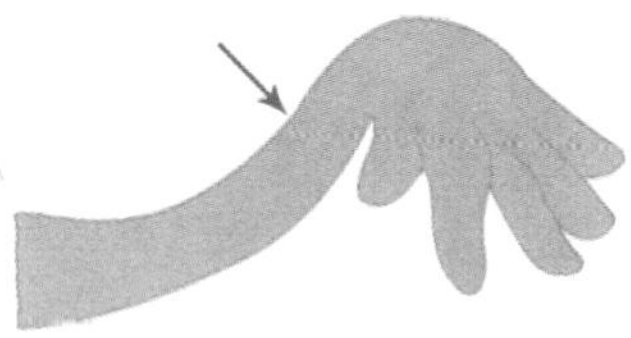

مِعْصَم/رُسْغ
miʿṣam\ruskh

Xx

x-ray

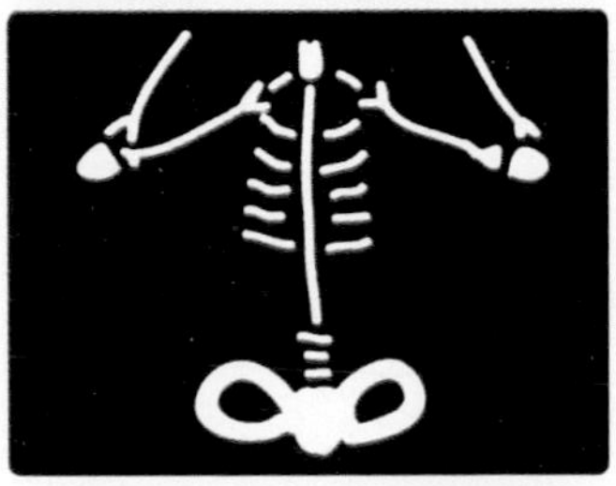

أَشِعَّةُ أَكْس
’ashiʿʿatu ’aks

xylophone

alkhashabiyyah الْخَشَبِيَّة

Yy

yacht

yakht يَخْت

yak

yāk يَاك

yard

sāhah سَاحَة

yellow

ʾaṣfar أَصْفَر

yoghurt

laban rāʾib لَبَن رَائِب

Zz

zebra

حِمَار الْوَحْش
ḥimārul waḥsh

zero

ṣifr صِفْر

zip

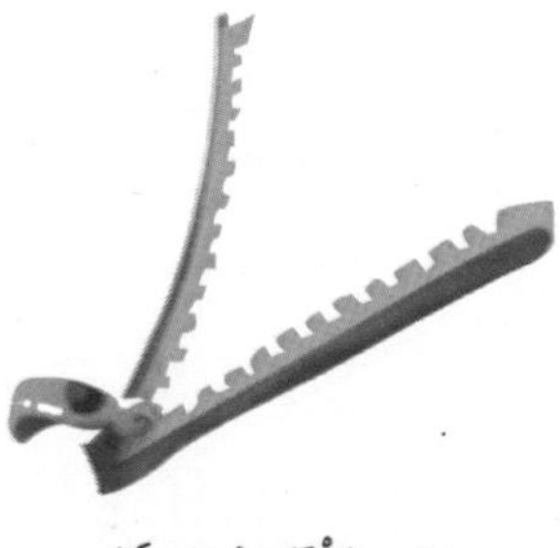

زِمَام مُنْزَلِق/سَحَّاب
zimām munzaliq\saḥḥāb

zodiac

دَائِرَةُ الْبُرُوج
dāʾiratul burūj

zoo

حَدِيْقَةُ الْحَيَوَان
ḥadīqatul ḥayawān